Easy Piano Selections

SCHOOL OF ROCK

MUSIC BY ANDREW LLOYD WEBBER | LYRICS BY GLEN[

CONTENTS

The musical works contained in this edition may not be publicly performed in a dramatic form or context except under license from The Really Useful Group Limited, 17 Slingsby Place, Longon WC2E 9AB

ISBN 978-1-5400-5655-9

Visit Hal Leonard Online at
www.halleonard.com

Contact us:
Hal Leonard
7777 West Bluemound Road
Milwaukee, WI 53213
Email: info@halleonard.com

In Europe, contact:
Hal Leonard Europe Limited
42 Wigmore Street
Marylebone, London, W1U 2RN
Email: info@halleonardeurope.com

In Australia, contact:
Hal Leonard Australia Pty. Ltd.
4 Lentara Court
Cheltenham, Victoria, 3192 Australia
Email: info@halleonard.com.au

WHEN I CLIMB TO THE TOP OF MOUNT ROCK

Music by ANDREW LLOYD WEBBER
Lyrics by GLENN SLATER

DEWEY:

I'll be strum-ming my axe ___ in a base-ment dive ___ with my
I'll be blow-ing out amps ___ play-ing sta-di-um shows ___ on my

to-tal-ly kick-ass band ___ when an ar-my of A ___ and R
sold-out ga-lac-tic tour. ___ And I'll blis-ter the ears ___ of the

men will ar-rive ___ with pens and con-tracts in hand. ___ And they'll
first thou-sand rows ___ and leave while they beg for ___ more. ___ Then I'll

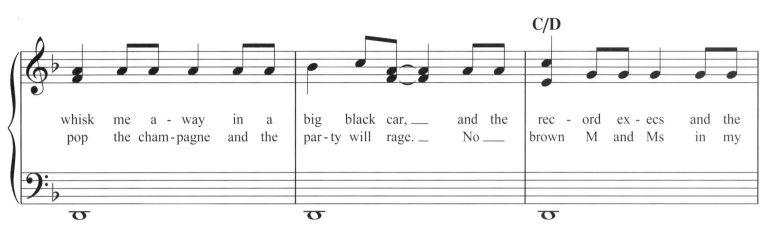

whisk me a-way in a big black car, ___ and the rec-ord ex-ecs and the
pop the cham-pagne and the par-ty will rage. ___ No ___ brown M and Ms in my

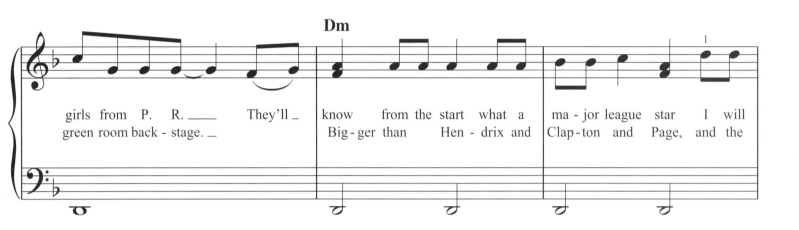

girls from P. R. ___ They'll ___ know from the start what a ma-jor league star I will
green room back-stage. ___ Big-ger than Hen-drix and Clap-ton and Page, and the

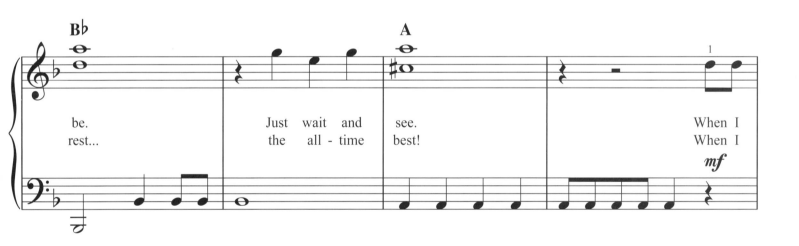

be. Just wait and see. When I
rest... the all-time best! When I

climb to the top of Mount Rock and I'm there star-ing down from the
climb to the top of Mount Rock and I'm perched at the up-per-most

4

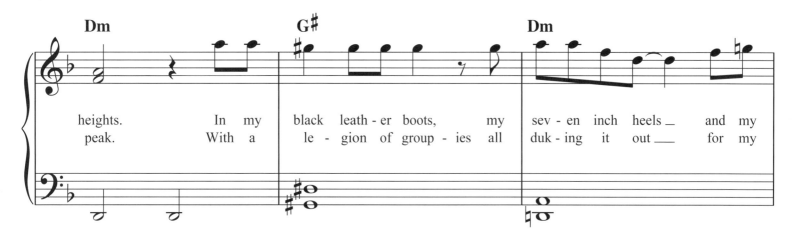

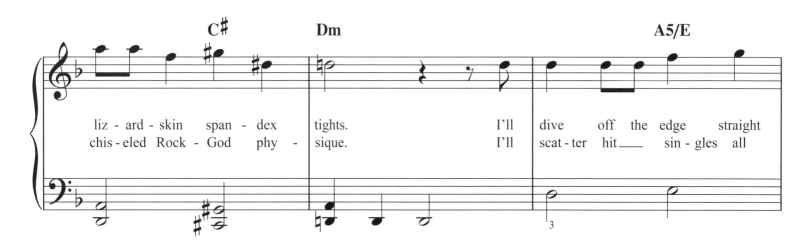

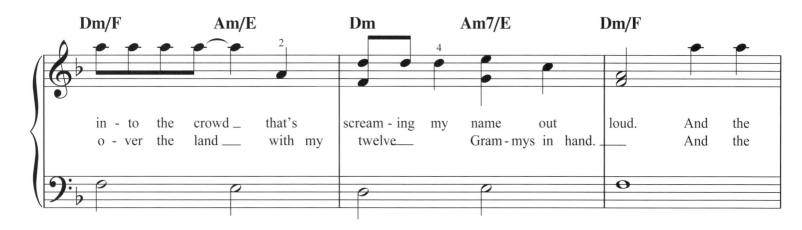

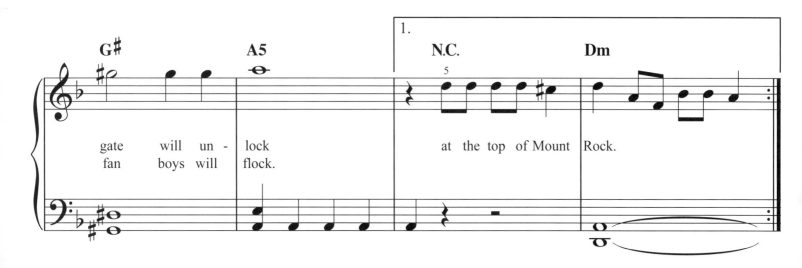

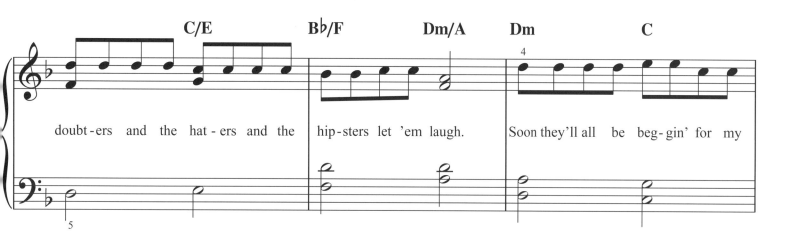

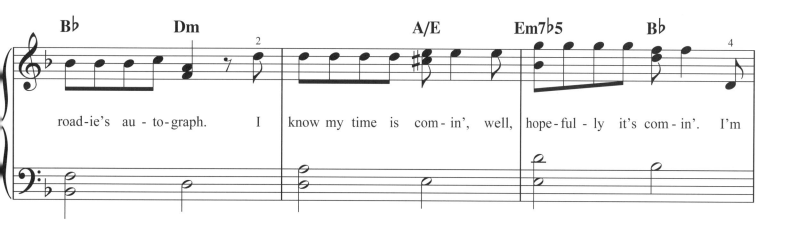

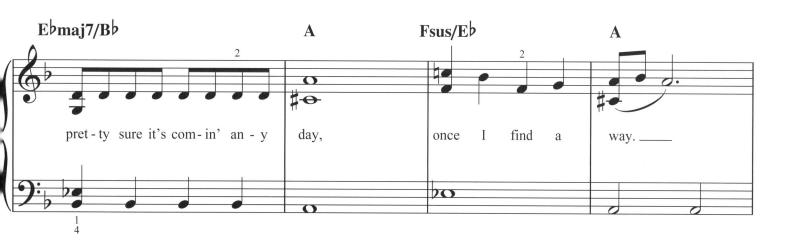

Tempo I

Then the dreams that I've had _____ since the day I turned ten _____ will be

mf

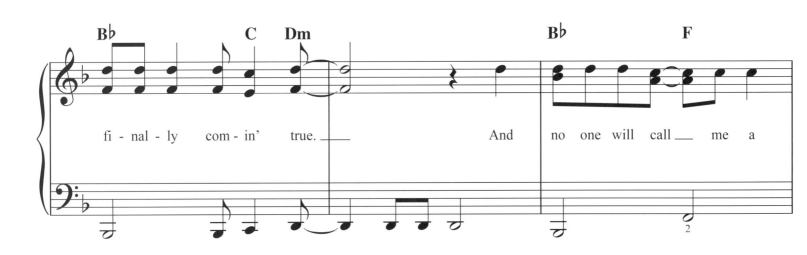

fi - nal - ly com - in' true. _____ And no one will call _____ me a

los - er a - gain _____ or tell me what I can't do. _____ So I'll

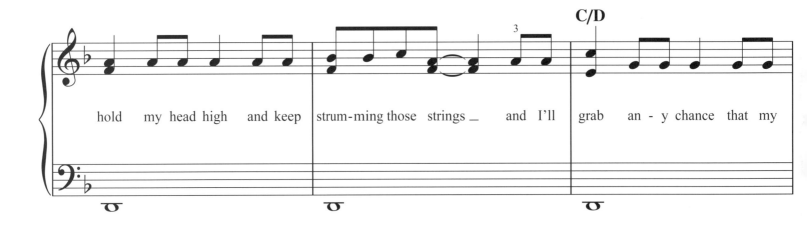

hold my head high and keep strum-ming those strings _____ and I'll grab an - y chance that my

des-ti-ny brings _ I'll _ rise and I'll rise and I'll rise on the wings of my

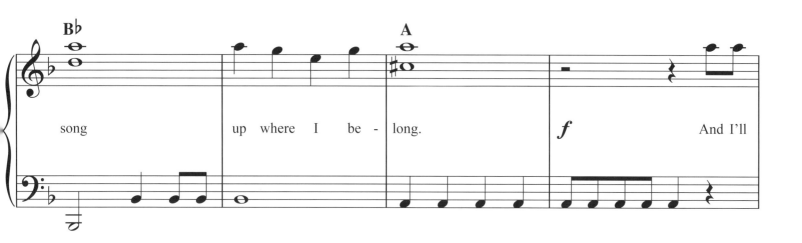

song up where I be - long. *f* And I'll

climb to the top of Mount Rock and be part of that heav-en-ly scene. With

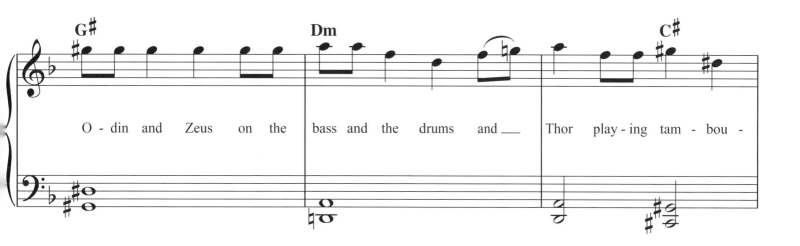

O - din and Zeus on the bass and the drums and _ Thor play-ing tam - bou -

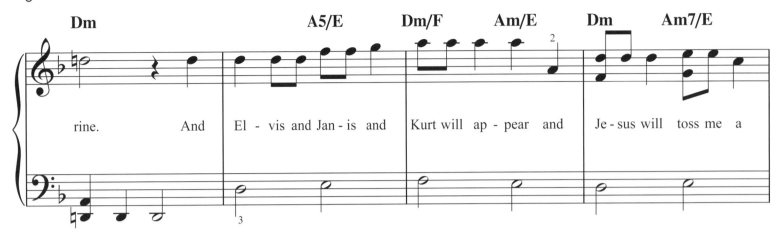

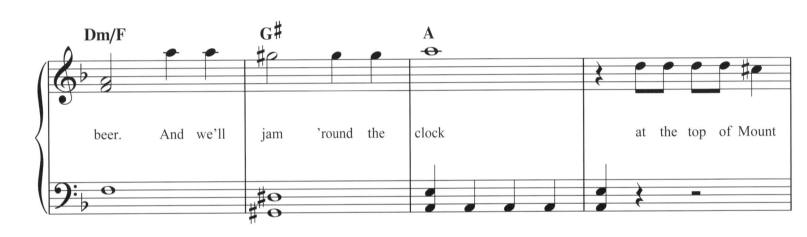

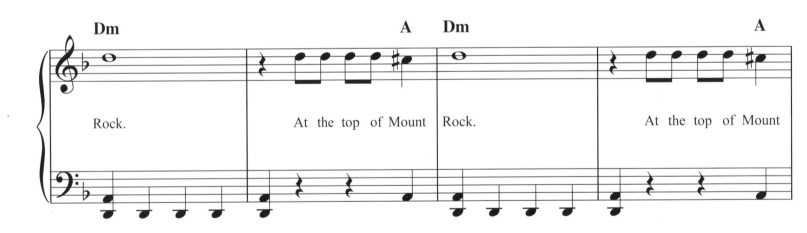

HERE AT HORACE GREEN

Music by ANDREW LLOYD WEBBER
Lyrics by GLENN SLATER

Precisely

ROSALIE:

Here at Hor - ace Green, our
At our hal - lowed school, the

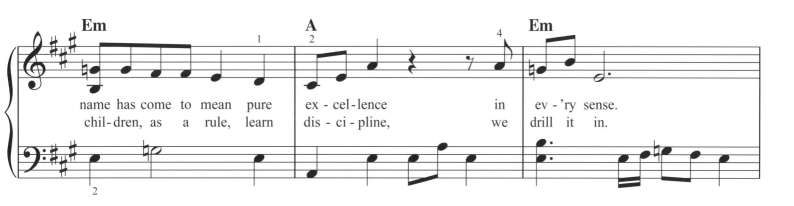

name has come to mean pure
chil - dren, as a rule, learn

ex - cel - lence   in   ev - 'ry sense.
dis - ci - pline,   we   drill it in.

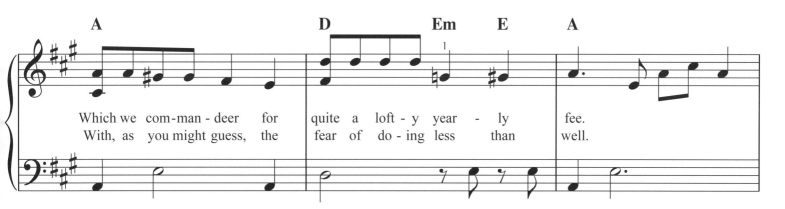

Which we com - man - deer   for
With, as you might guess, the

quite a loft - y year - ly   fee.
fear of do - ing less than   well.

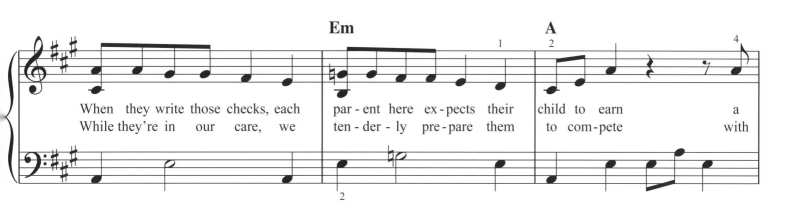

When they write those checks, each
While they're in our care, we

par - ent here ex - pects their
ten - der - ly pre - pare them

child to earn   a
to com - pete   with

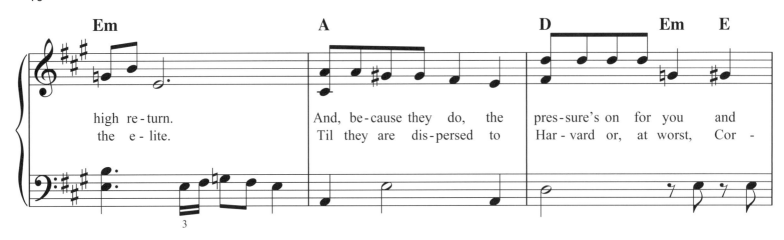

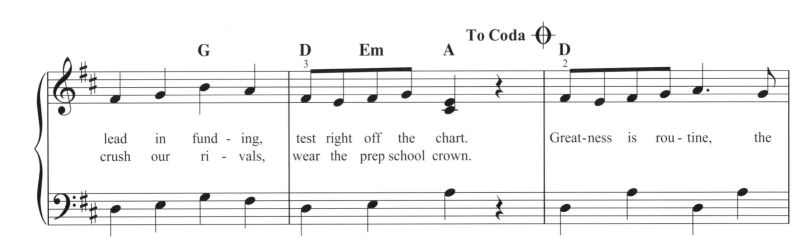

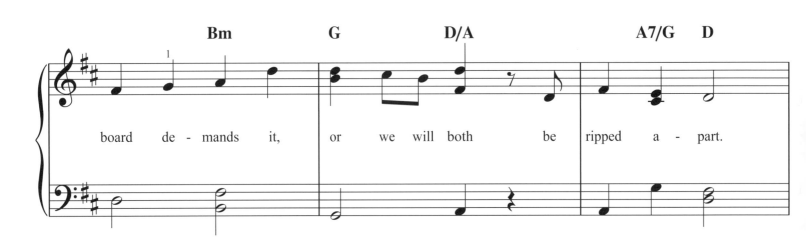

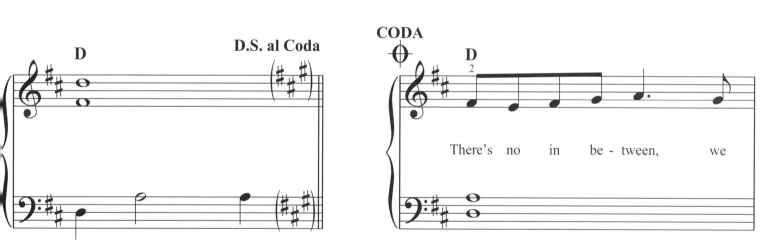

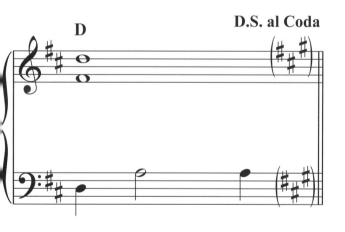

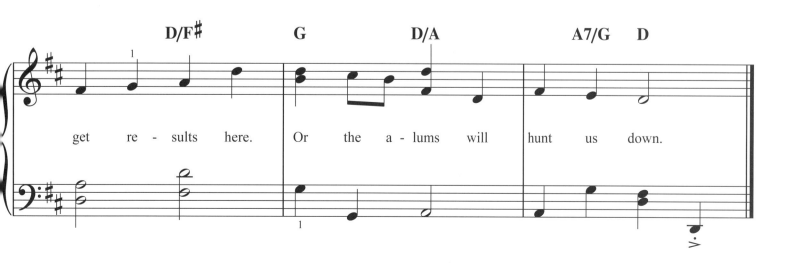

There's no in be - tween, we

get re - sults here. Or the a - lums will hunt us down.

HORACE GREEN ALMA MATER

Music by ANDREW LLOYD WEBBER
Lyrics by GLENN SLATER

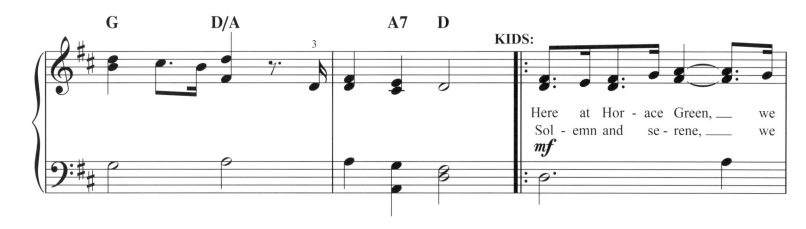

KIDS:

Here at Hor - ace Green, ___ we

Sol - emn and se - rene, ___ we

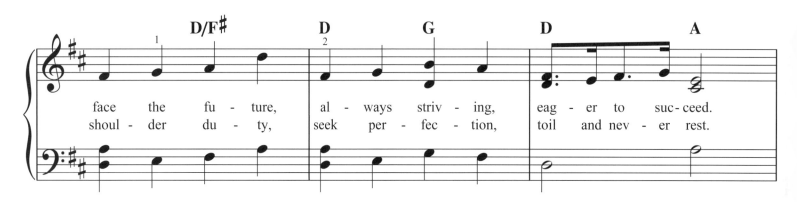

face the fu - ture, al - ways striv - ing, eag - er to suc - ceed.

shoul - der du - ty, seek per - fec - tion, toil and nev - er rest.

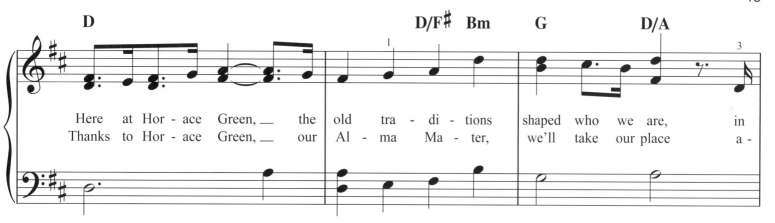

Here at Hor - ace Green, __ the old tra - di - tions shaped who we are, in

Thanks to Hor - ace Green, __ our Al - ma Ma - ter, we'll take our place a -

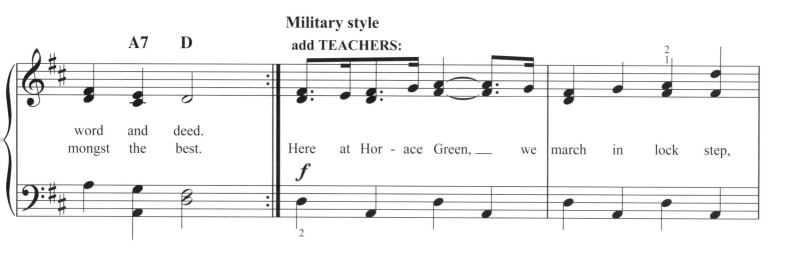

Military style
add TEACHERS:

word and deed.

mongst the best.

Here at Hor - ace Green, __ we march in lock step,

ev - er up - ward, des - tined to a - chieve. Here at Hor - ace Green, __ we

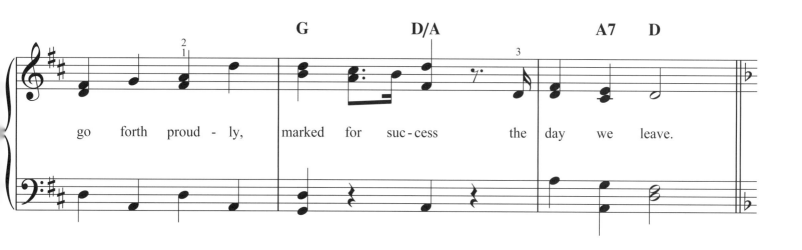

go forth proud - ly, marked for suc - cess the day we leave.

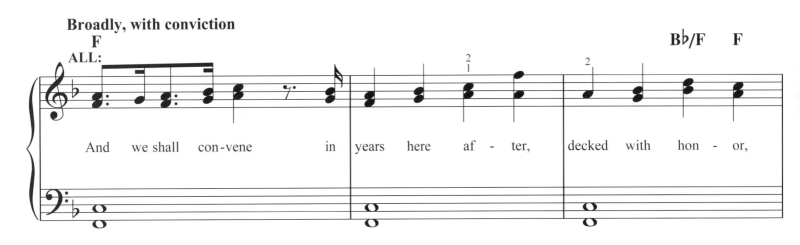

Broadly, with conviction

And we shall con-vene in years here af - ter, decked with hon - or,

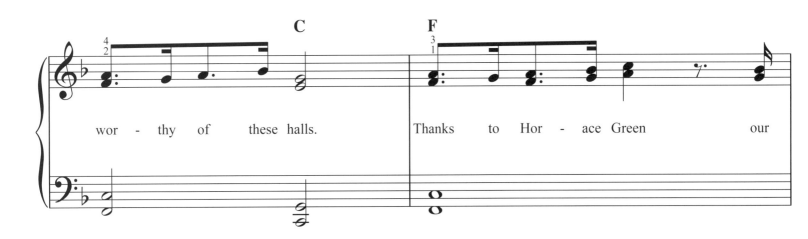

wor - thy of these halls. Thanks to Hor - ace Green our

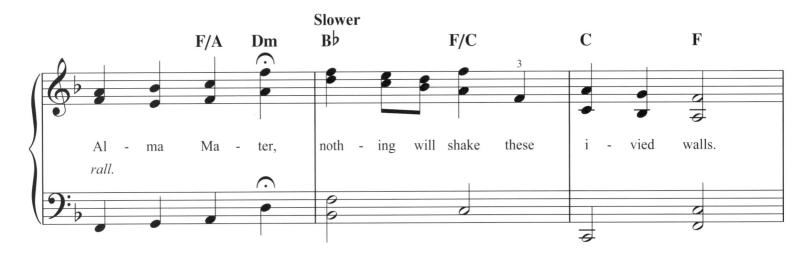

Slower

Al - ma Ma - ter, noth - ing will shake these i - vied walls.

rall.

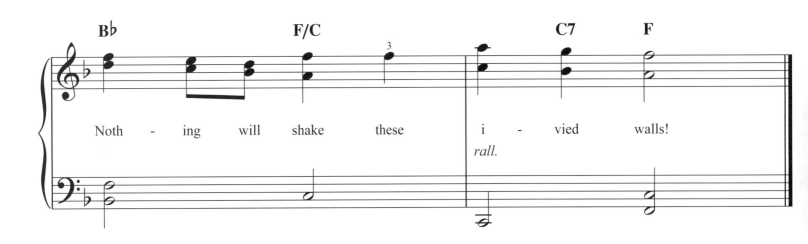

Noth - ing will shake these i - vied walls!

rall.

YOU'RE IN THE BAND

Music by ANDREW LLOYD WEBBER
Lyrics by GLENN SLATER

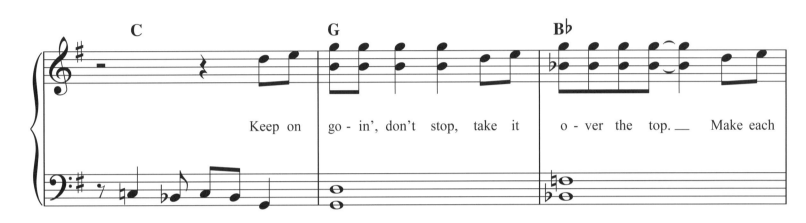

Keep on go-in', don't stop, take it o-ver the top.__ Make each

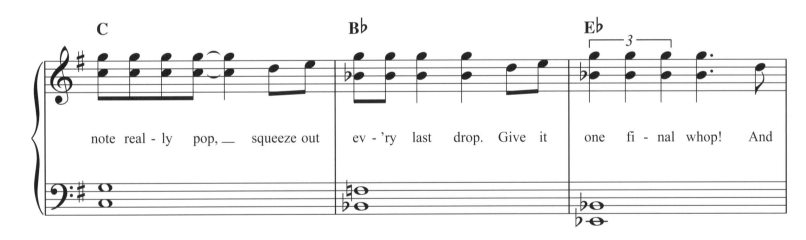

note real-ly pop,__ squeeze out ev-'ry last drop. Give it one fi-nal whop! And

yes! You're in the band.__

Turn a cel - lo this way, — and it's

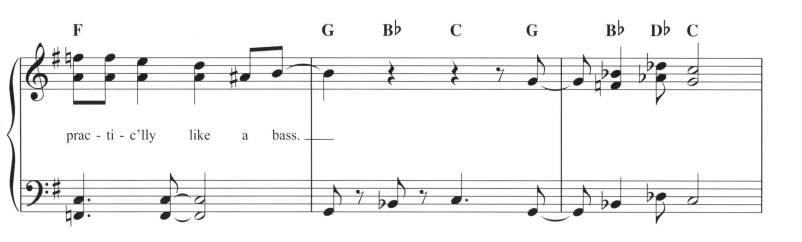

F · · · · · · · · · · · · · · · · · G Bb C G Bb Db C

prac - ti - c'lly like a bass. —

G Bb C Bb G

Pop the strings when you play and

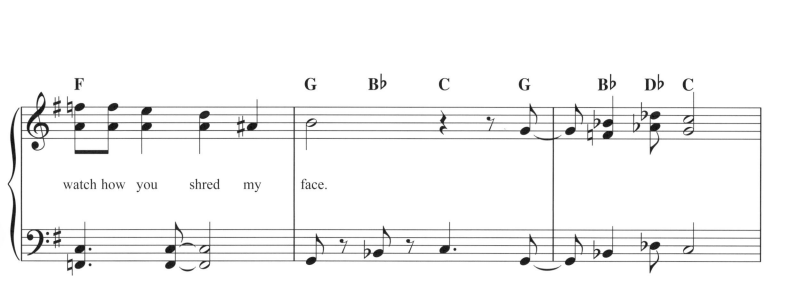

F G Bb C G Bb Db C

watch how you shred my face.

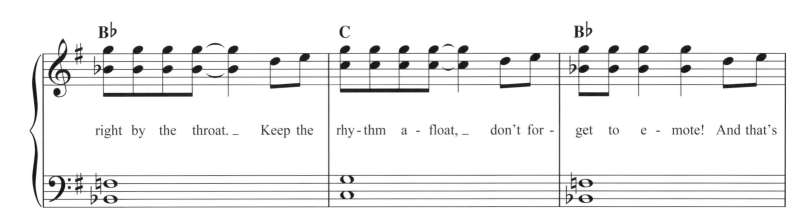

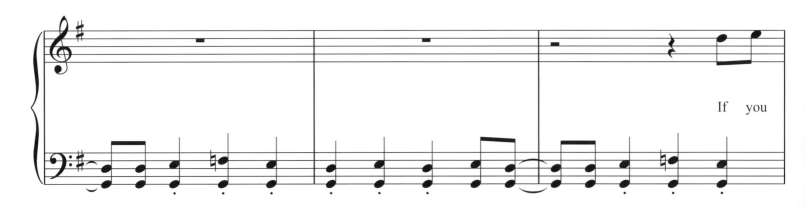

play the pi - an - o, you can play the keys.___

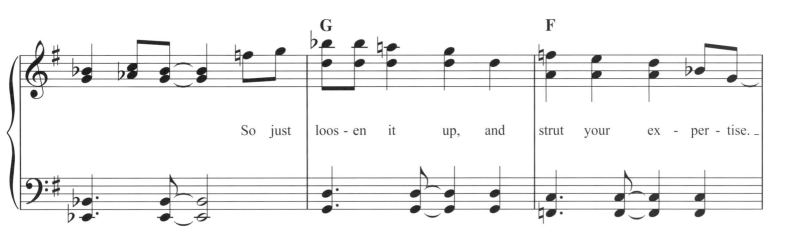

So just loos - en it up, and strut your ex - per - tise.__

___ Take a look at this mu - sic and

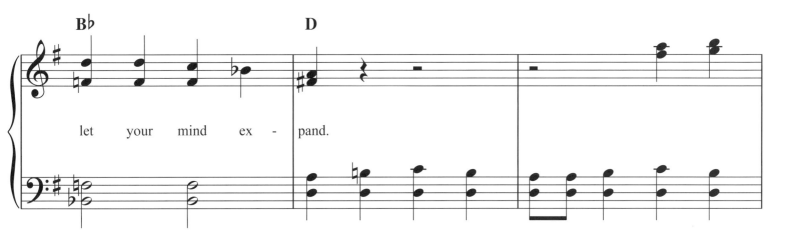

let your mind ex - pand.

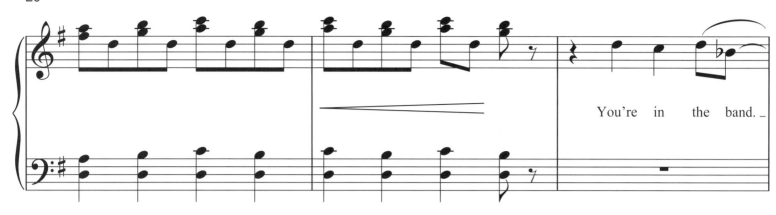

slow - ly turn up the heat. ___ And now

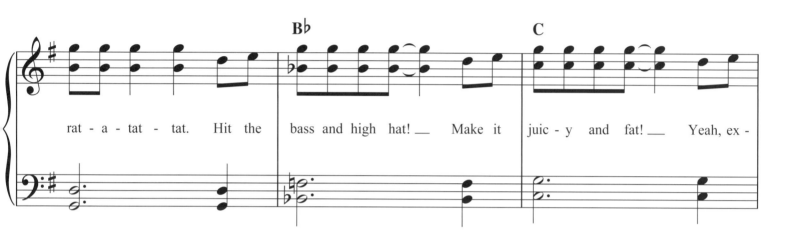

rat - a - tat - tat. Hit the bass and high hat! ___ Make it juic - y and fat! ___ Yeah, ex -

act - ly like that! And now shut it down flat... You're in the band! _

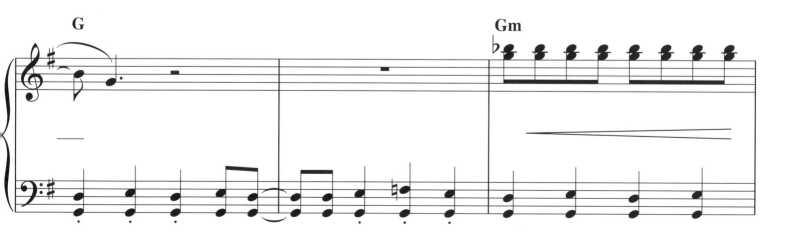

Now re - peat af - ter me, ___ "I pledge al - le - giance to the band." _

___ "And I prom-ise to give ___ Mis - ter

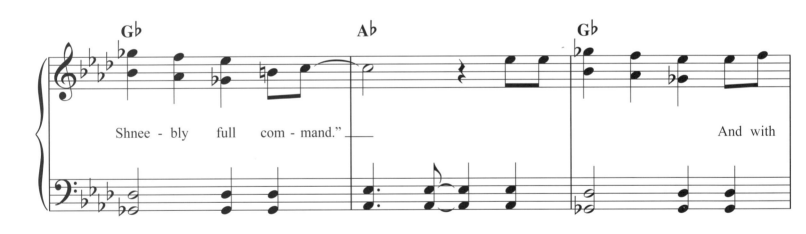

Shnee - bly full com - mand." ___ And with

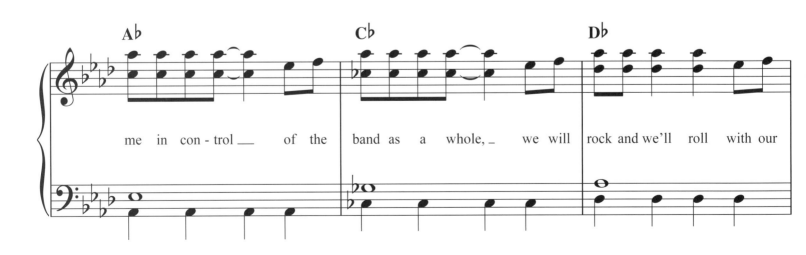

me in con - trol ___ of the band as a whole, _ we will rock and we'll roll with our

heart and our soul. If you're in, raise your hand! _ I'm in the

band. I'm in _____ the band. I'm in the band. I'm in _____ the

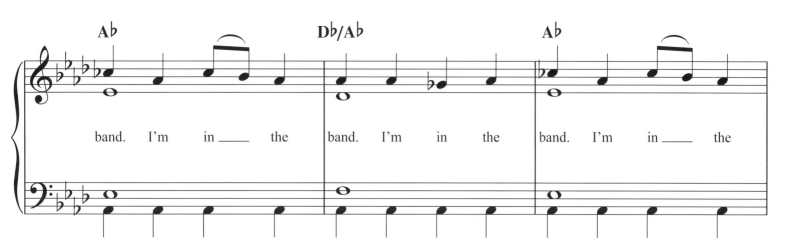

band. You're in the band. We're in _____ the band. You're in the

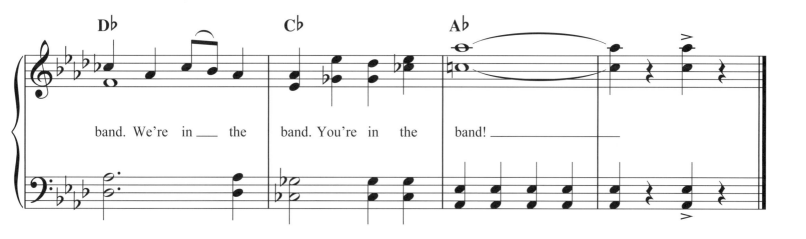

band. We're in _____ the band. You're in the band! _____

CHILDREN OF ROCK

Music by ANDREW LLOYD WEBBER
Lyrics by GLENN SLATER

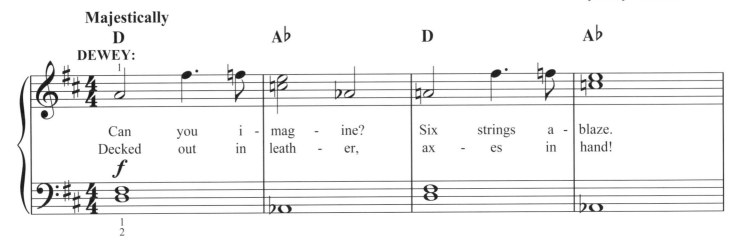

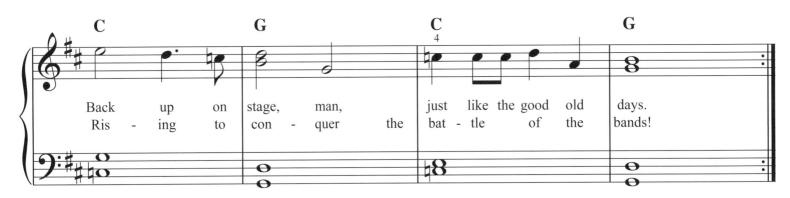

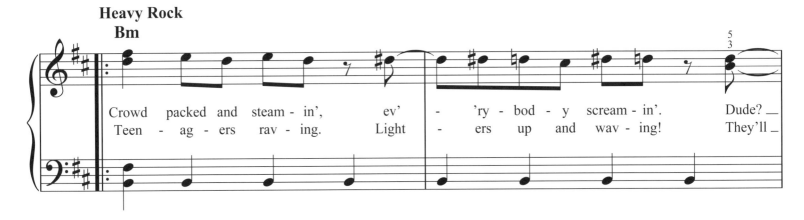

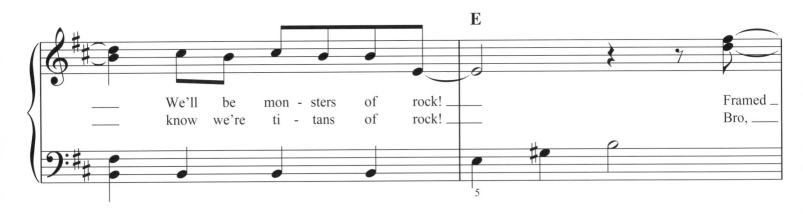

in the spot - light, bask - in' in that hot light. Ass -
let's get to it, you know ___ you wan - na do it. Let's ___

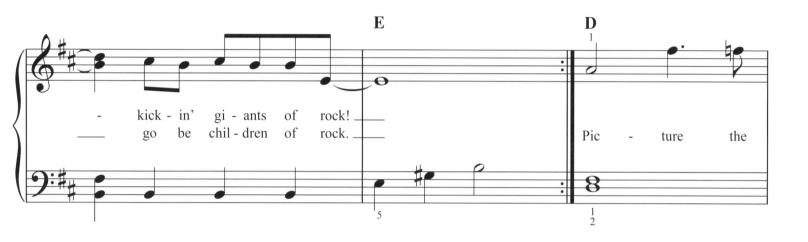

- kick - in' gi - ants of rock! ___
___ go be chil - dren of rock. ___ Pic - ture the

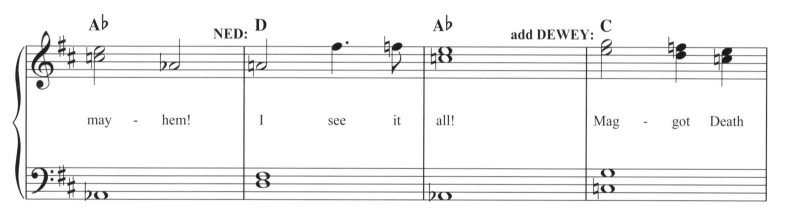

may - hem! I see it all! Mag - got Death

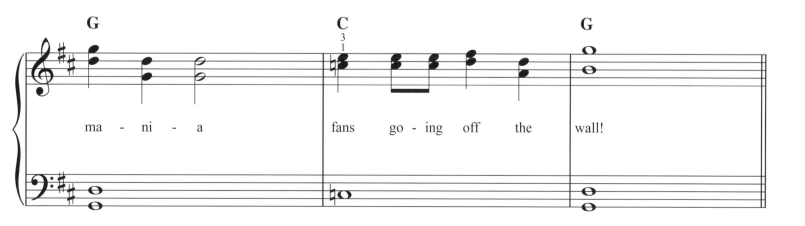

ma - ni - a fans go - ing off the wall!

Bm

DEWEY:

Amps o - ver - load - in', en - er - gy ex - plod - in'! Us ___
Rag - ing and reel - ing. Noth - ing like the feel - ing when ___

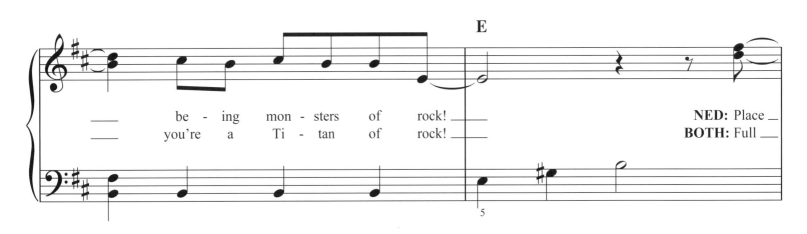

E

___ be - ing mon - sters of rock! ___ **NED:** Place ___
___ you're a Ti - tan of rock! ___ **BOTH:** Full ___

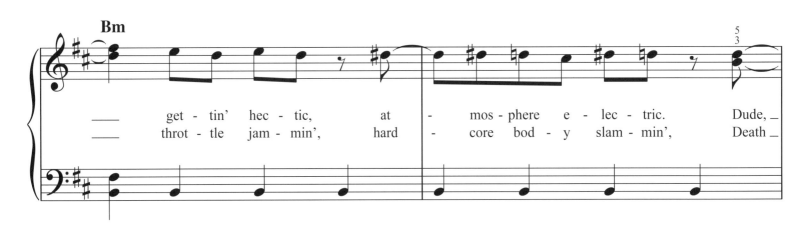

Bm

___ get - tin' hec - tic, at - mos - phere e - lec - tric. Dude, ___
___ throt - tle jam - min', hard - core bod - y slam - min', Death ___

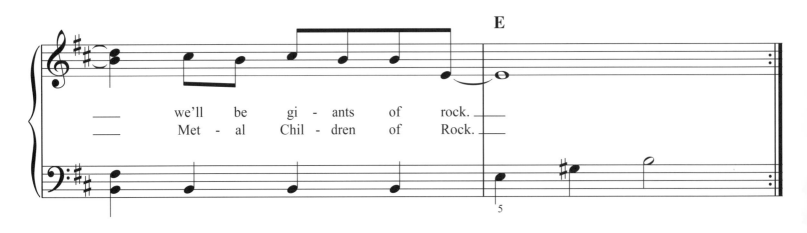

E

___ we'll be gi - ants of rock. ___
Met - al Chil - dren of Rock.

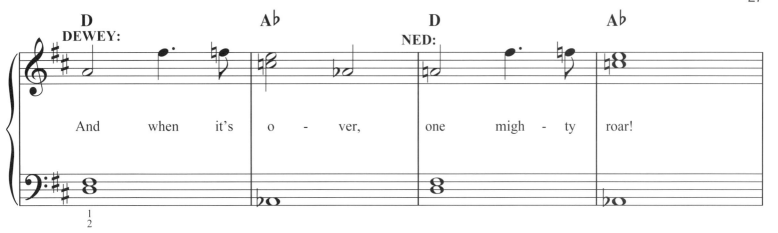

DEWEY: And when it's o - ver,   **NED:** one migh - ty roar!

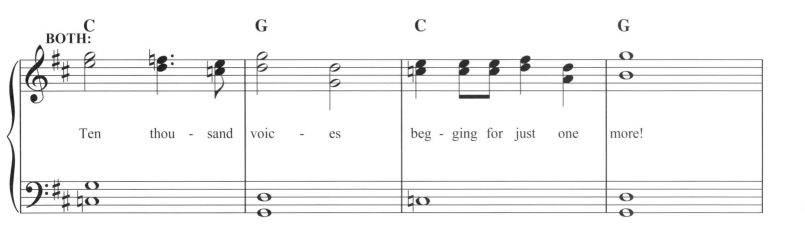

BOTH: Ten thou - sand voic - es   beg - ging for just one more!

IF ONLY YOU WOULD LISTEN

Music by ANDREW LLOYD WEBBER
Lyrics by GLENN SLATER

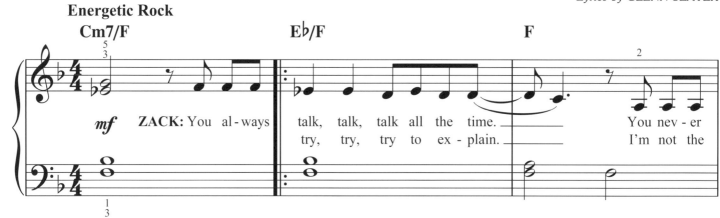

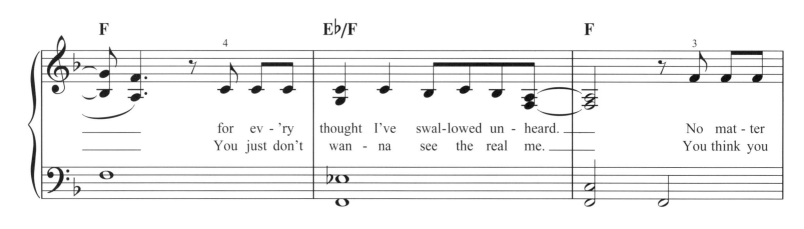

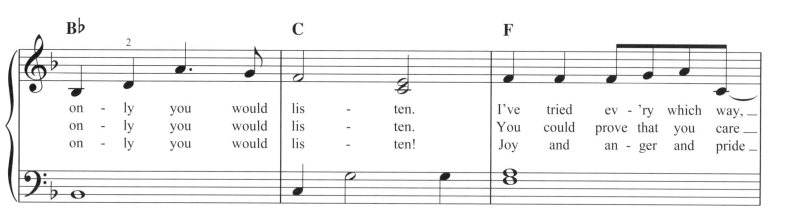

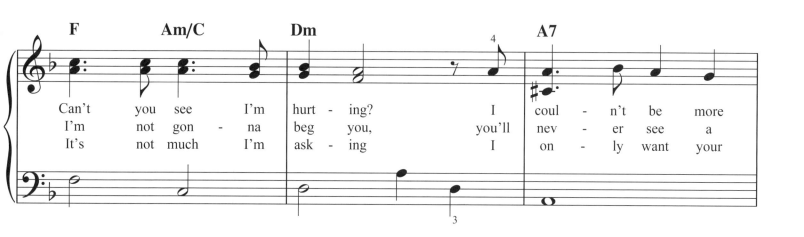

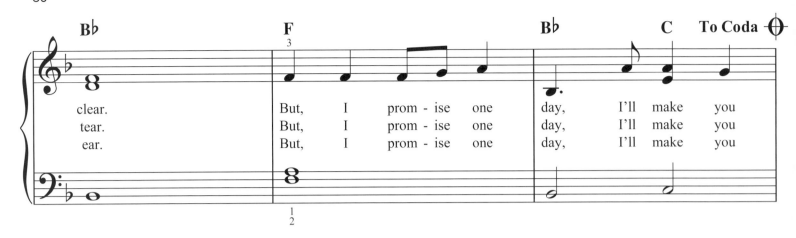

clear.
tear.
ear.

But, I prom-ise one day, I'll make you

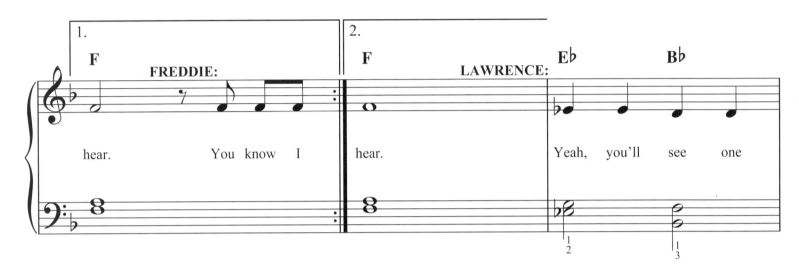

1.

FREDDIE:

hear. You know I

2.

LAWRENCE:

hear. Yeah, you'll see one

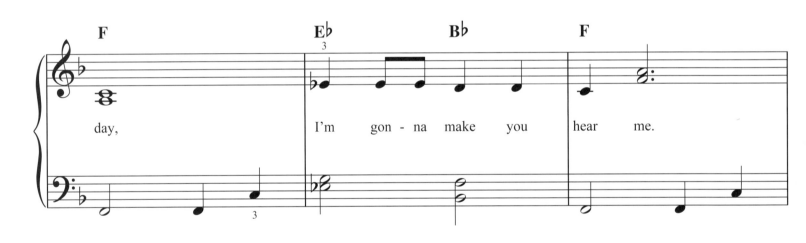

day, I'm gon-na make you hear me.

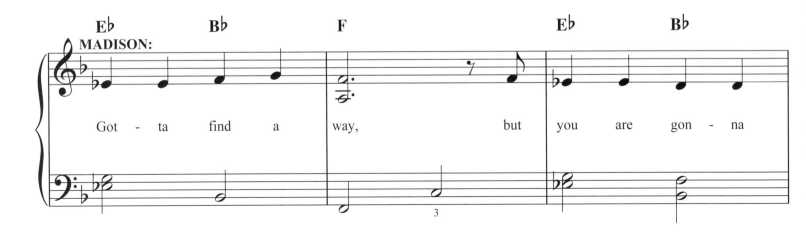

MADISON:

Got - ta find a way, but you are gon - na

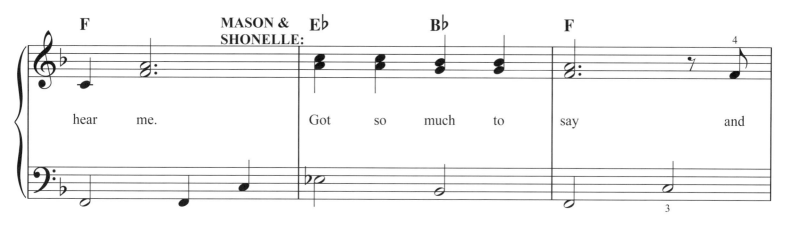

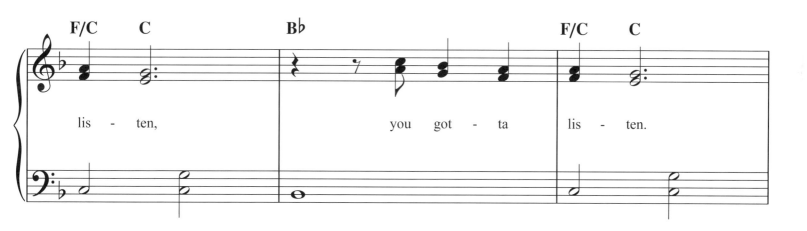

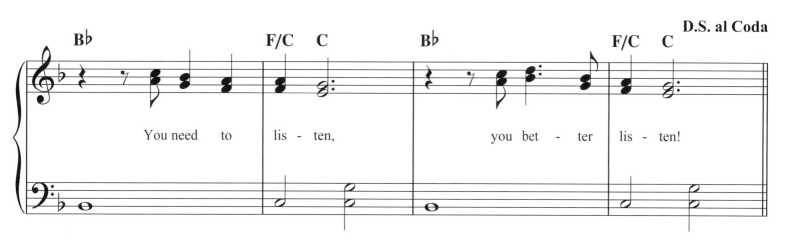

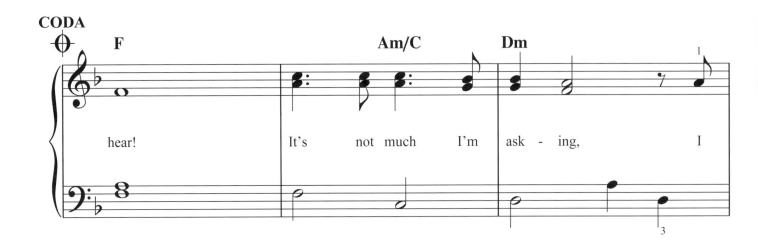

CODA

hear! It's not much I'm ask - ing, I

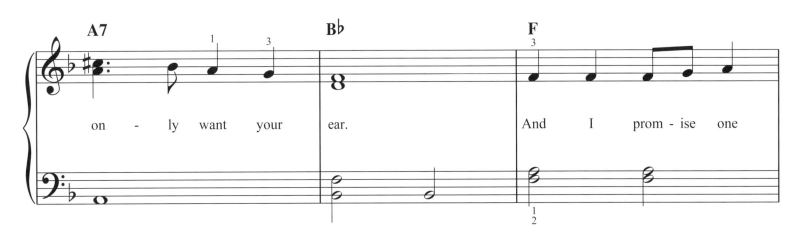

on - ly want your ear. And I prom - ise one

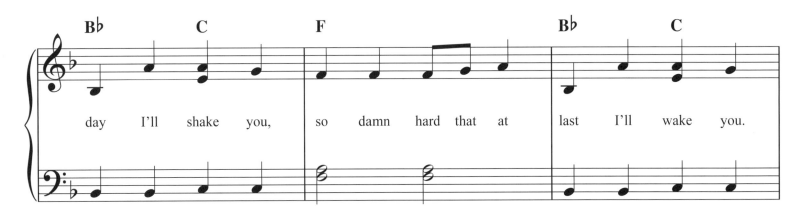

day I'll shake you, so damn hard that at last I'll wake you.

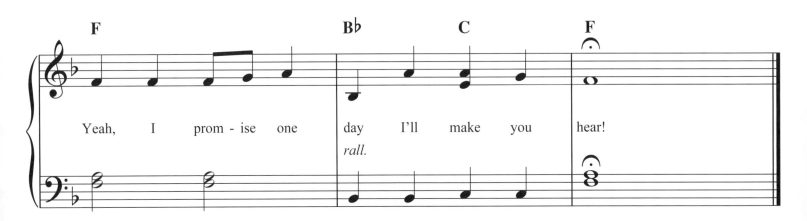

Yeah, I prom - ise one day I'll make you hear!

rall.

STICK IT TO THE MAN

Music by ANDREW LLOYD WEBBER
Lyrics by GLENN SLATER

Medium Blues Rock

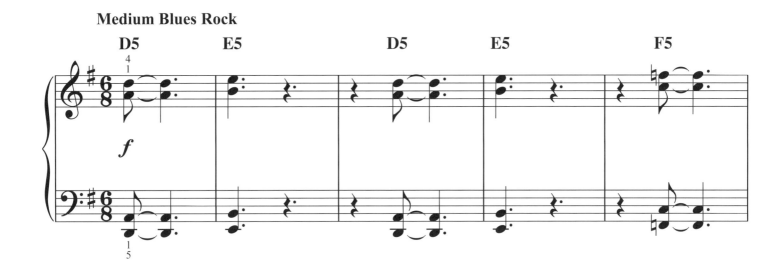

DEWEY:

1., 3. When the world has screwed you ___ and crushed you in its fist,

2. Par - ents o - ver work ya? ___ Stick it to the man!

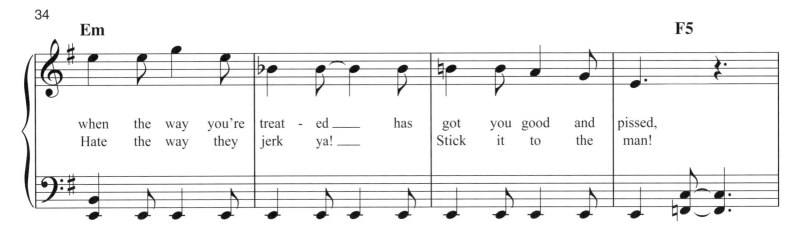

Em ... **F5**

when the way you're treat- ed ___ has got you good and pissed,
Hate the way they jerk ya! ___ Stick it to the man!

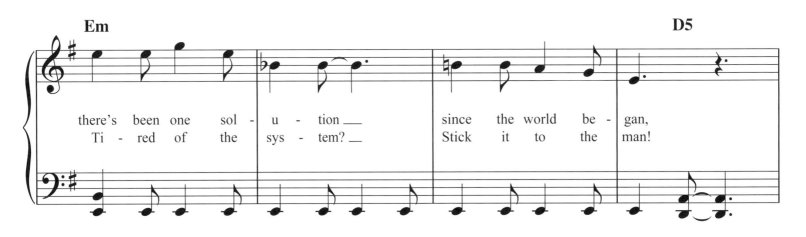

Em ... **D5**

there's been one sol - u - tion ___ since the world be - gan,
Ti - red of the sys - tem? ___ Stick it to the man!

To Coda ⊕

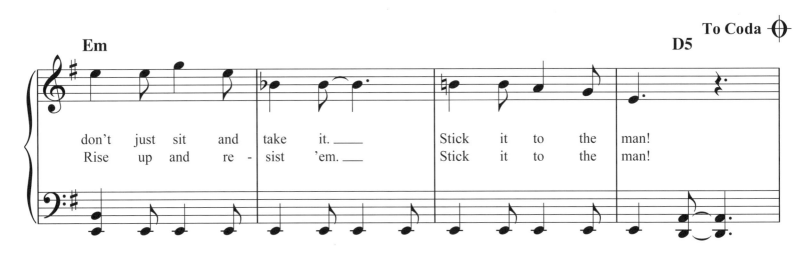

Em ... **D5**

don't just sit and take it. ___ Stick it to the man!
Rise up and re - sist 'em. ___ Stick it to the man!

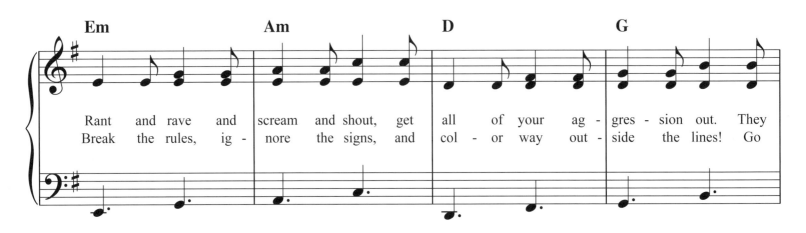

Em ... **Am** ... **D** ... **G**

Rant and rave and scream and shout, get all of your ag - gres - sion out. They
Break the rules, ig - nore the signs, and col - or way out - side the lines! Go

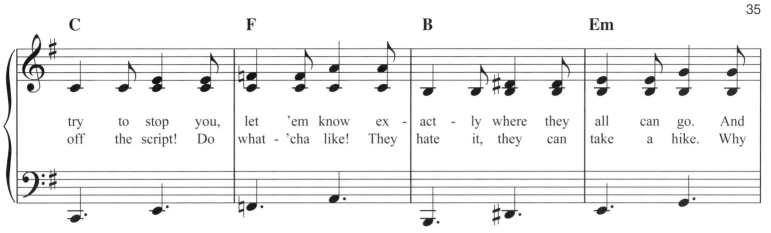

try to stop you, let 'em know ex - act - ly where they all can go. And
off the script! Do what - 'cha like! They hate it, they can take a hike. Why

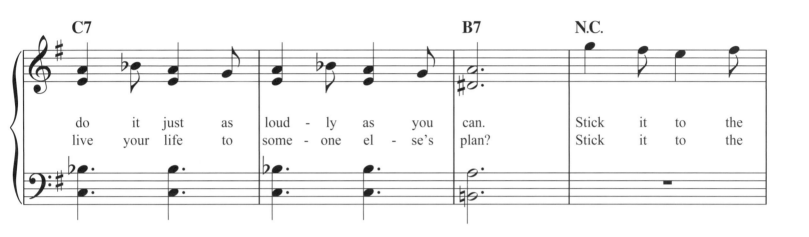

do it just as loud - ly as you can. Stick it to the
live your life to some - one el - se's plan? Stick it to the

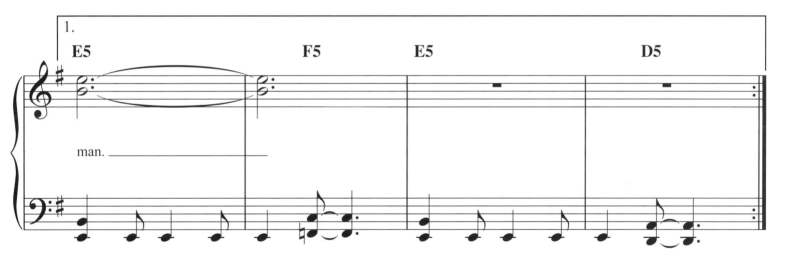

1.

man. _____

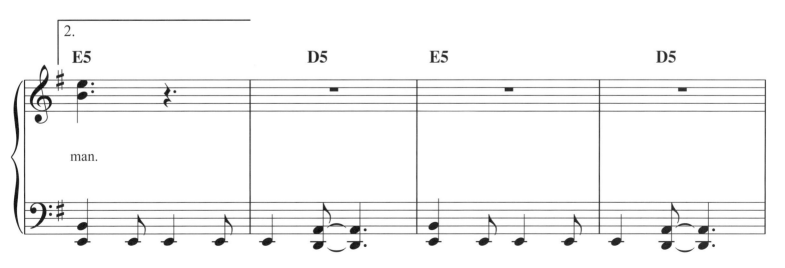

2.

man.

E5

(Spoken:) Pissed at pol - i - ti - cians? _ (Sung:) Stick it to the man!

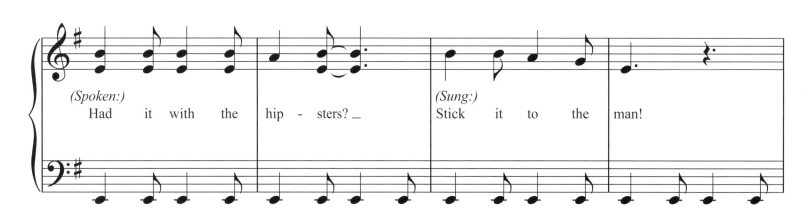

(Spoken:) Had it with the hip - sters? _ (Sung:) Stick it to the man!

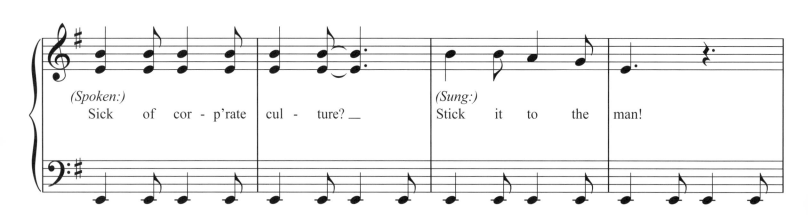

(Spoken:) Sick of cor - p'rate cul - ture? _ (Sung:) Stick it to the man!

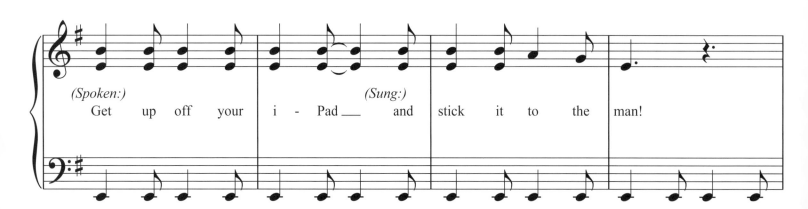

(Spoken:) Get up off your i - Pad __ (Sung:) and stick it to the man!

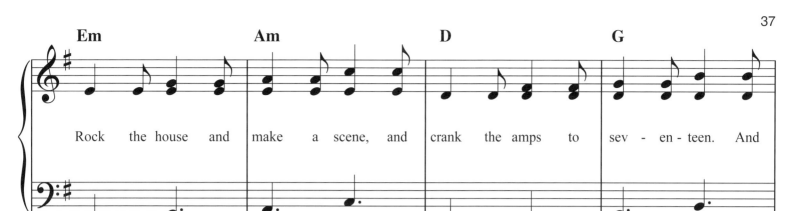

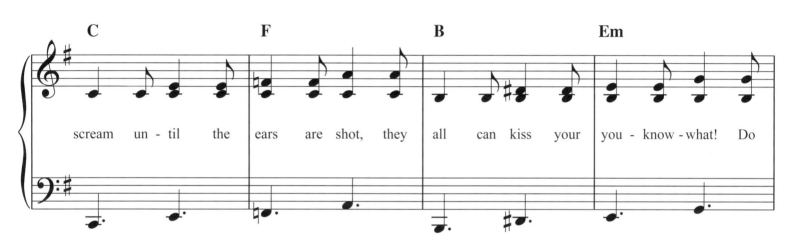

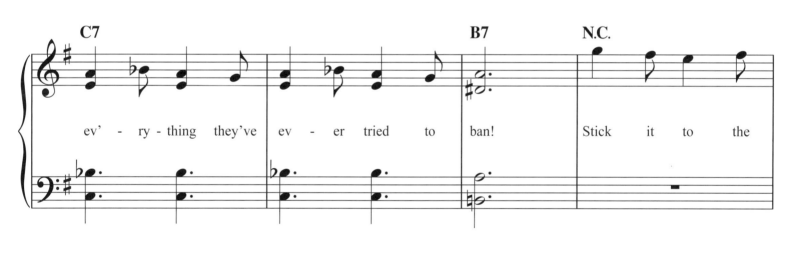

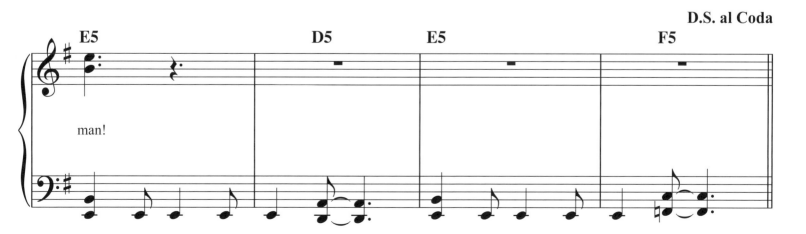

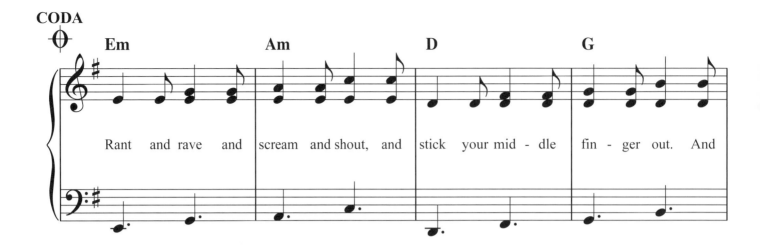

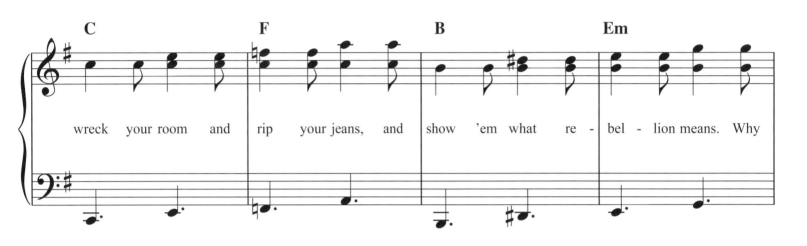

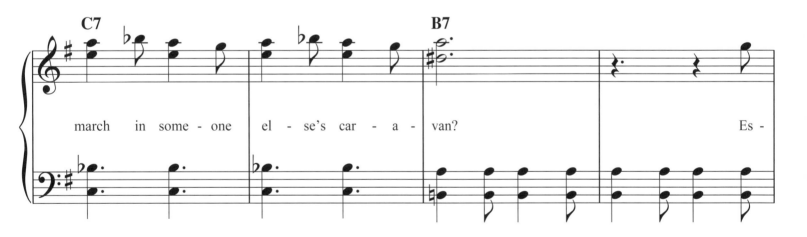

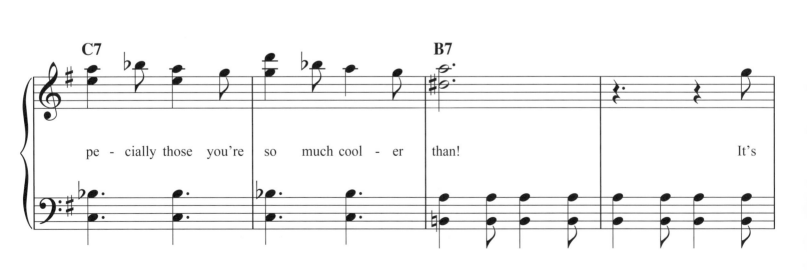

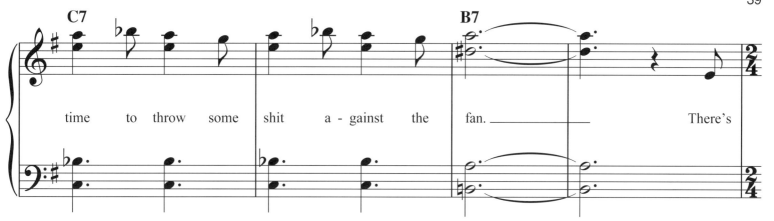

time to throw some shit a - gainst the fan. _____ There's

Very broadly

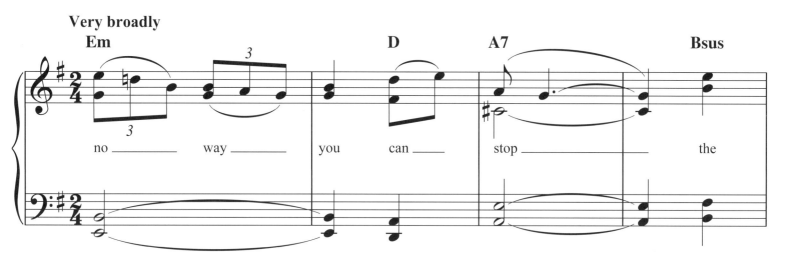

no _____ way _____ you can _____ stop _____ the

Tempo I

School of _____ Rock!

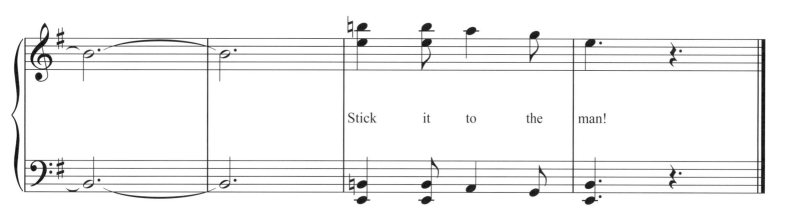

Stick it to the man!

TIME TO PLAY

Music by ANDREW LLOYD WEBBER
Lyrics by GLENN SLATER

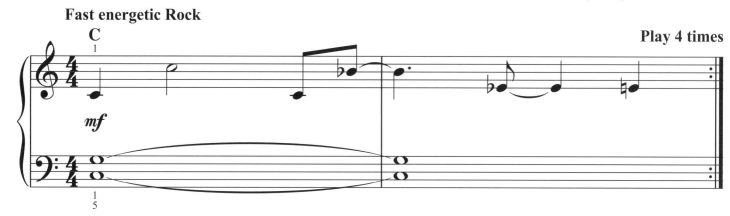

SUMMER:

Hey! ain't got all day! Get mov - ing!
You! Go on and cue the light board.

You! No one comes through that door!
You! Show them the new hot move.

No dis - trac - tions, no de - lays ___ This is for our
Look re - bel - lious, act more crude. ___ Bring your best bad

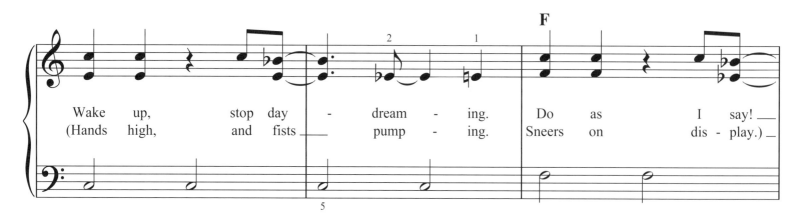

Wake up, stop day - dream - ing. Do as I say! __
(Hands high, and fists pump - ing. Sneers on dis - play.) __

__ Get those gui - tars __ scream - ing,
__ Let's get this joint __ jump - ing!

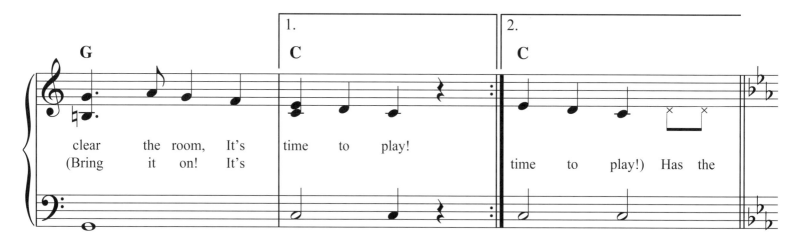

clear the room, It's time to play!
(Bring it on! It's time to play!) Has the

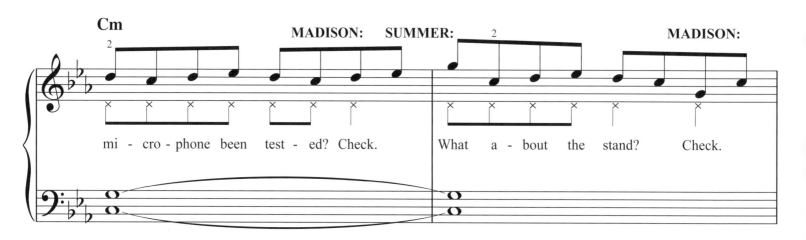

MADISON: SUMMER:
mi - cro - phone been test - ed? Check. What a - bout the stand? Check.

MADISON:

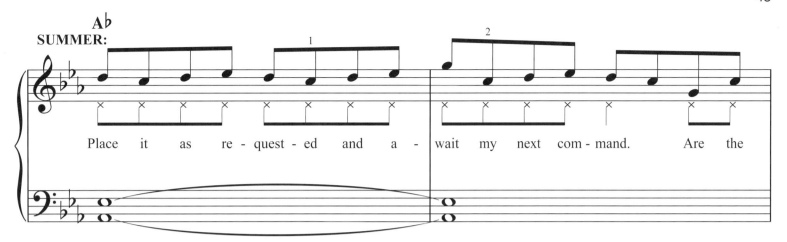

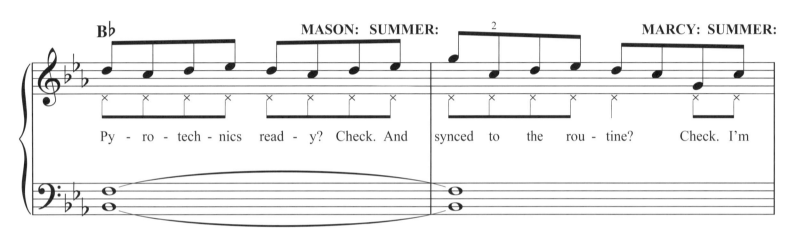

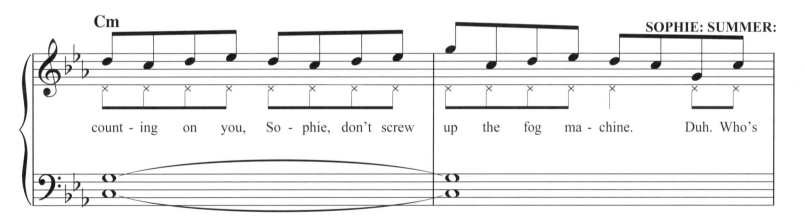

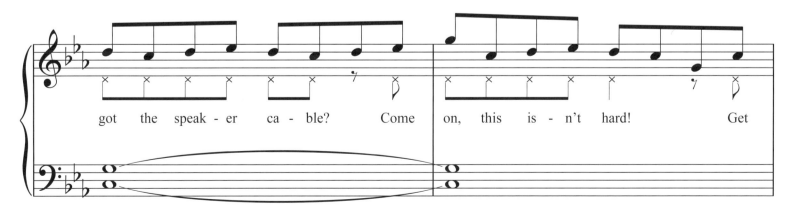

44

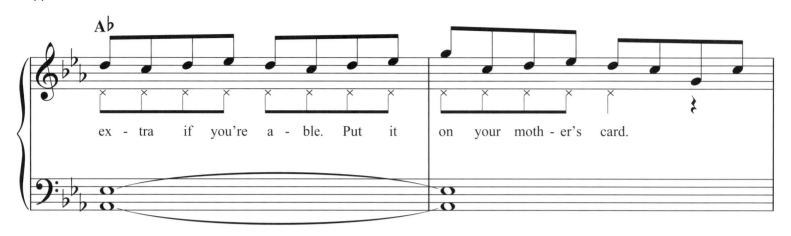

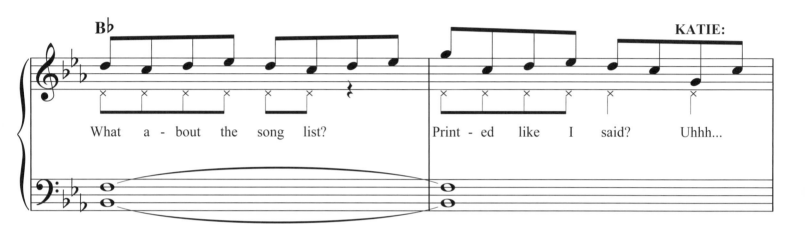

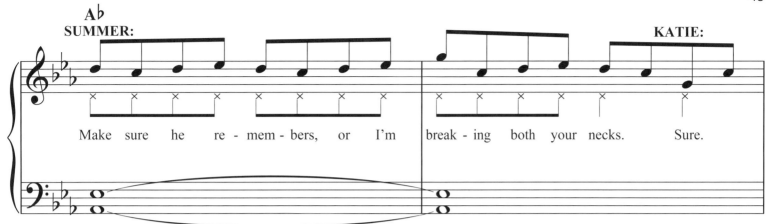

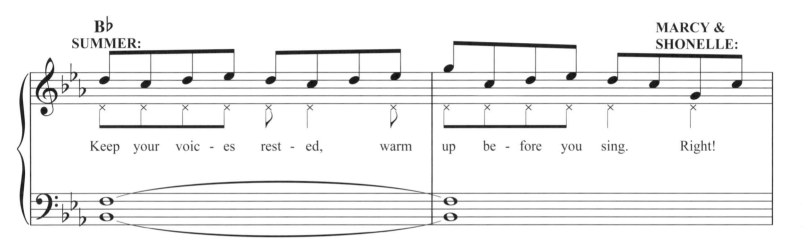

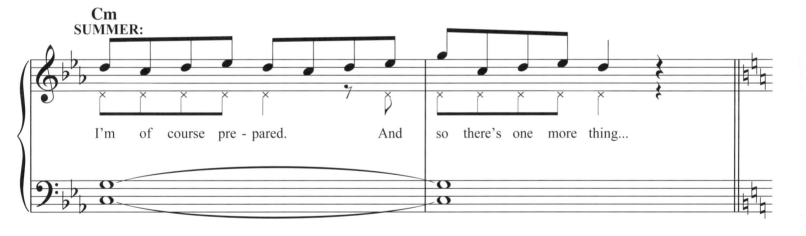

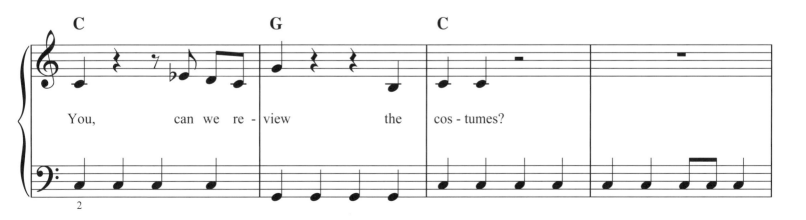

Jeez! Don't be a tease. Let's go!

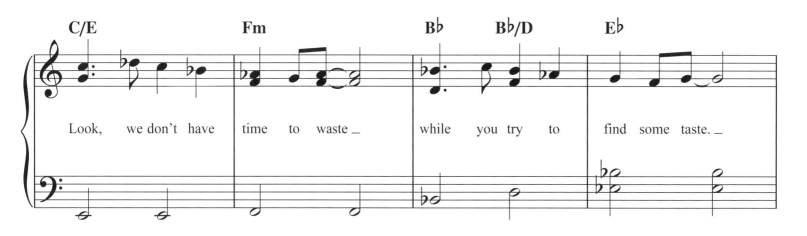

Look, we don't have time to waste ___ while you try to find some taste. ___

BILLY:
Fine! Here's the de - sign. Hell no.

ALL KIDS:
Amps cranked, and drums ___
Don't slack, there's no ___

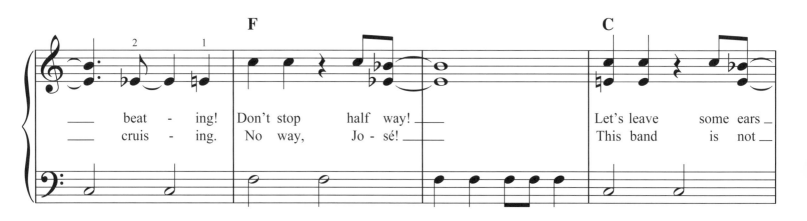

___ beat - ing! Don't stop half way! ___ Let's leave some ears ___
___ cruis - ing. No way, Jo - sé! ___ This band is not ___

WHERE DID THE ROCK GO?

Music by ANDREW LLOYD WEBBER
Lyrics by GLENN SLATER

Gently, in 2

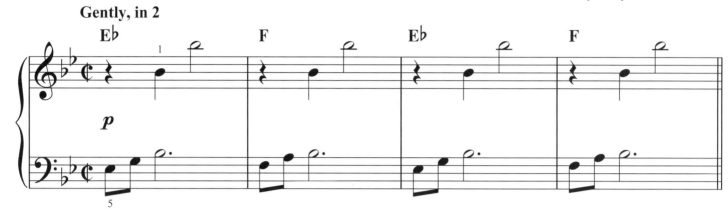

ROSALIE:

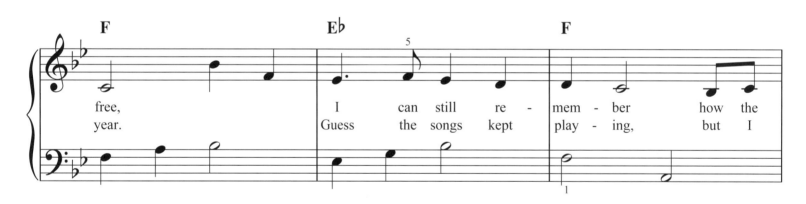

Back when I was young - er, wild and bold and
Some - how I got old - er, year by bus - y

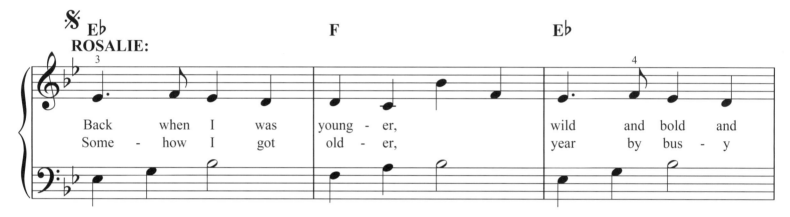

free, I can still re - mem - ber how the
year. Guess the songs kept play - ing, but I

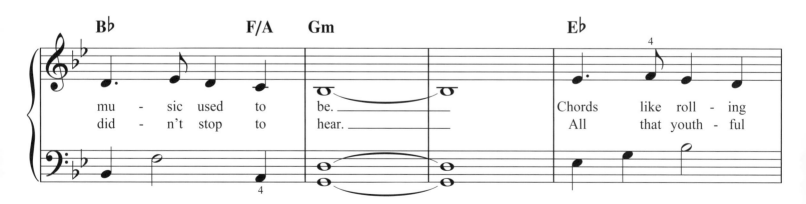

mu - sic used to be. Chords like roll - ing
did - n't stop to hear. All that youth - ful

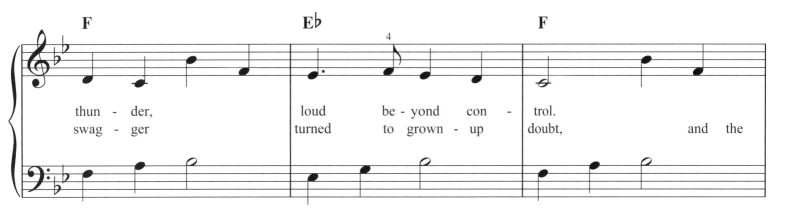

thun - der,   loud   be - yond con - trol.

swag - ger   turned   to grown - up doubt,   and the

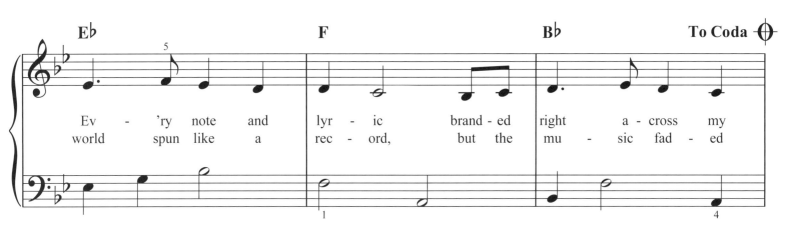

Ev - 'ry note and   lyr - ic   brand - ed   right   a - cross   my

world   spun like a   rec - ord,   but the   mu - sic fad - ed

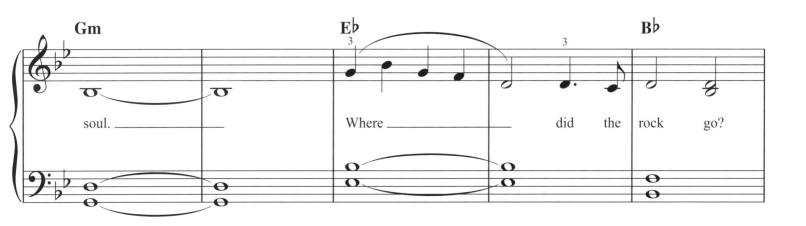

soul. _____   Where _____   did   the rock   go?

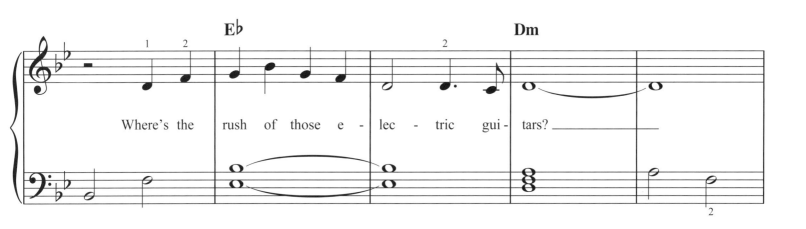

Where's the   rush of those e - lec - tric gui - tars? _____

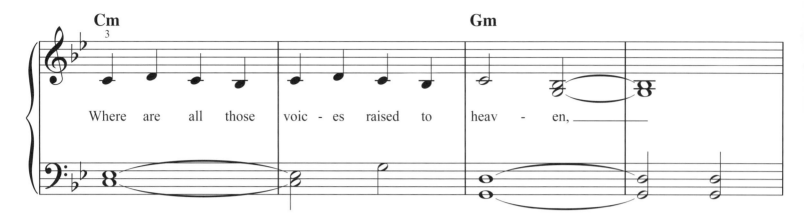

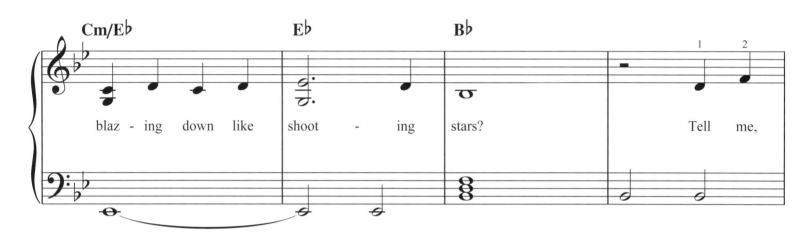

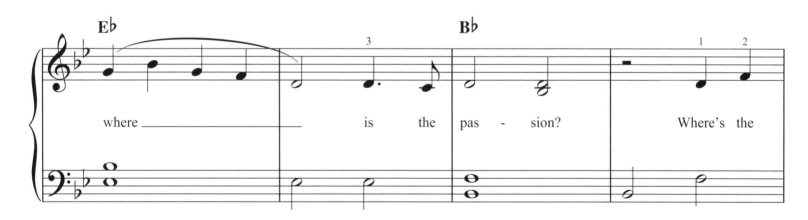

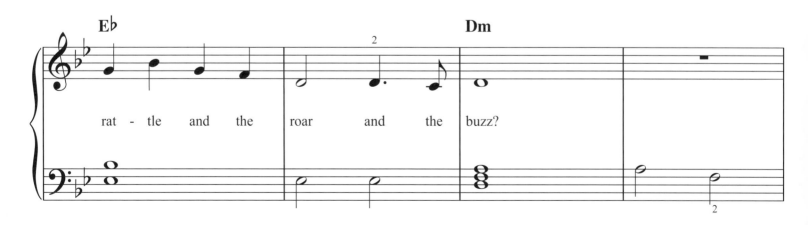

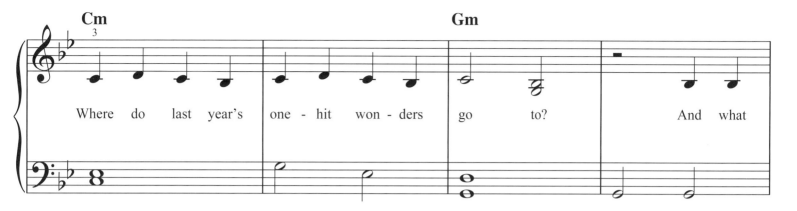

Where do last year's one-hit won-ders go to? And what

hap-pened to the girl I was? _____

D.S. al Coda

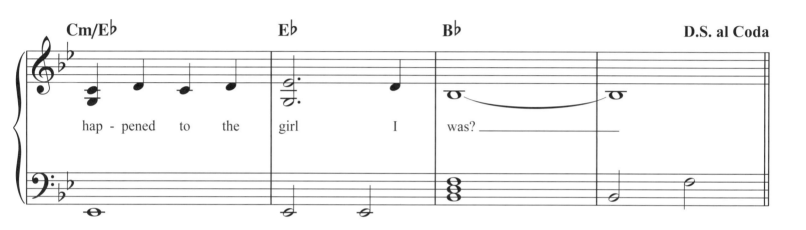

CODA

out. _____ Where _____ did the rock go?

mf

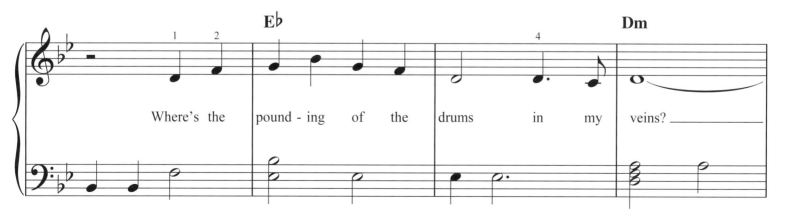

Where's the pound-ing of the drums in my veins? _____

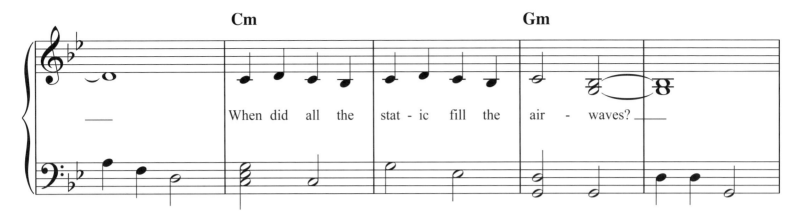

When did all the stat - ic fill the air - waves? ____

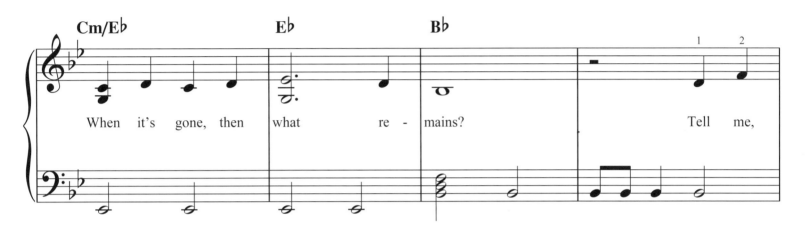

When it's gone, then what re - mains? Tell me,

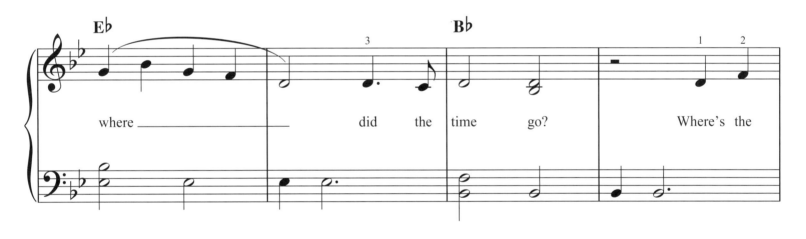

where _____ did the time go? Where's the

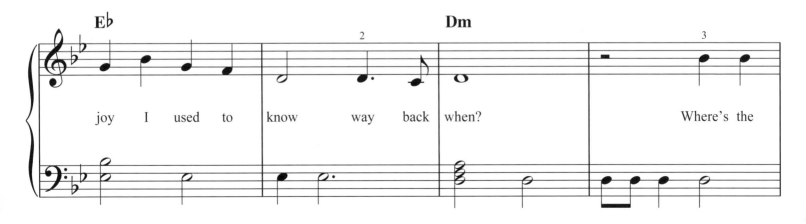

joy I used to know way back when? Where's the

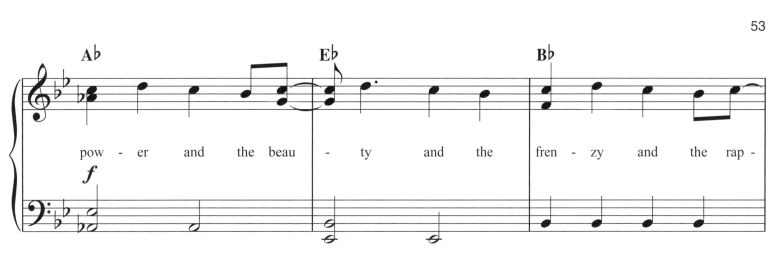

power and the beau - ty and the fren - zy and the rap -

- ture? Where's the ma - gic of the mo - ments on - ly

rock could ev - er cap - ture? Now the on - ly thing I'm hear -

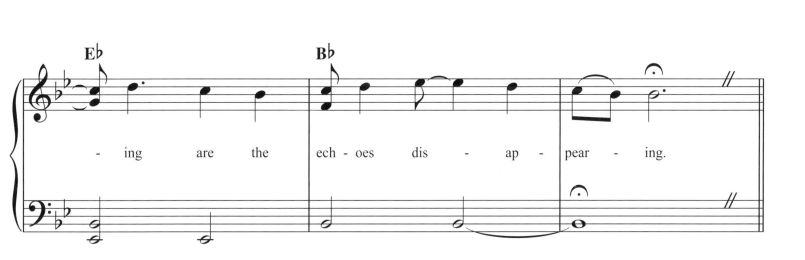

- ing are the ech - oes dis - ap - pear - ing.

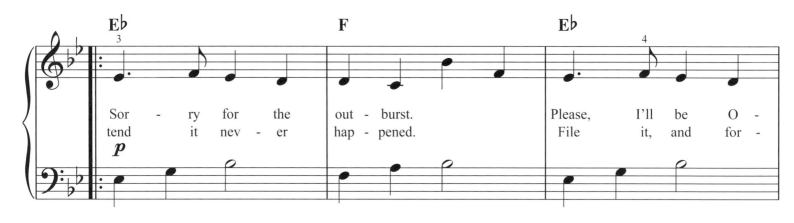

Sor - ry for the out - burst. Please, I'll be O -
tend it nev - er hap - pened. File it, and for -

p

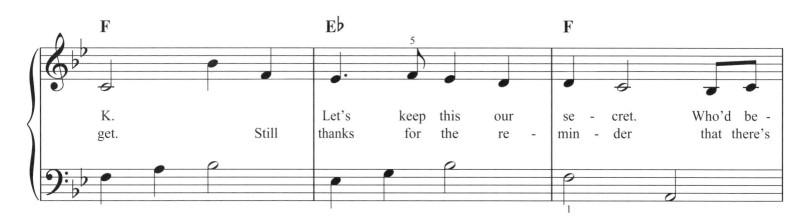

K. Still Let's keep this our se - cret. Who'd be -
get. thanks for the re - min - der that there's

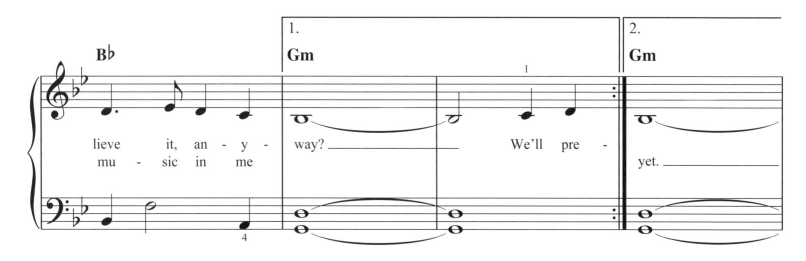

lieve it, an - y - way? We'll pre -
mu - sic in me yet.

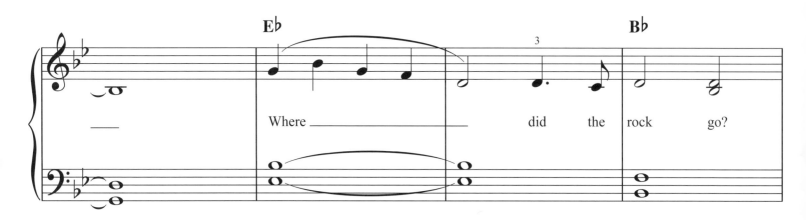

Where did the rock go?

All those feel - ings that I've learned to ig - nore?

If you flip the rec - ord and start o - ver,

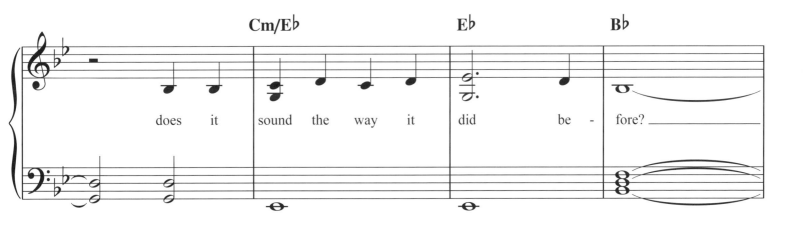

does it sound the way it did be - fore? _____

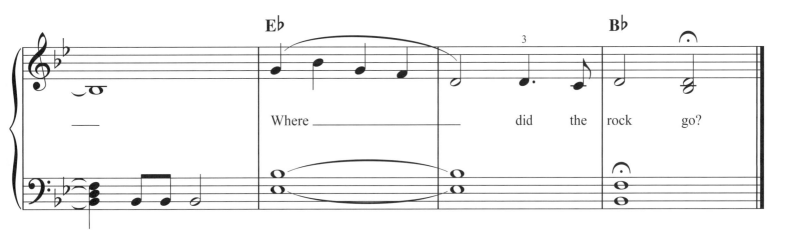

_____ Where _____ did the rock go?

IF ONLY YOU WOULD LISTEN
(Reprise)

Music by ANDREW LLOYD WEBBER
Lyrics by GLENN SLATER

Slow Gospel

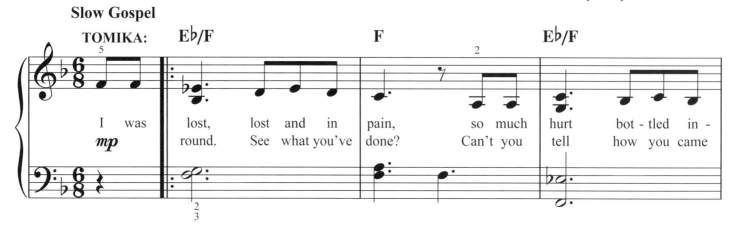

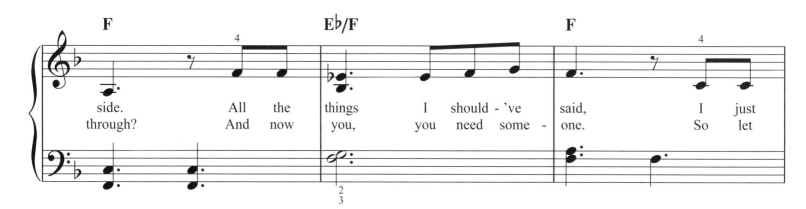

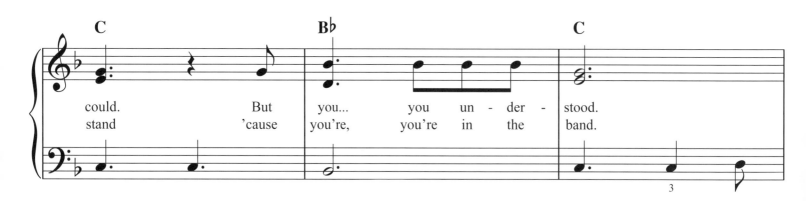

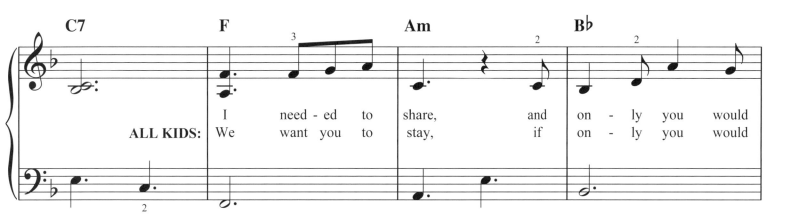

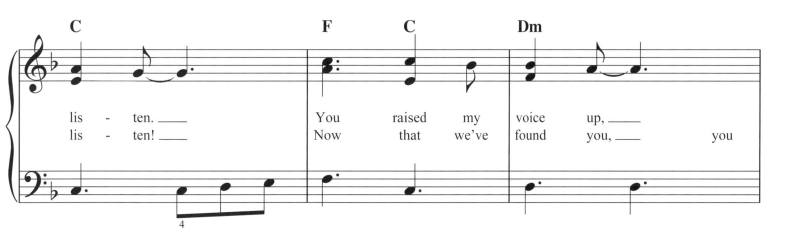

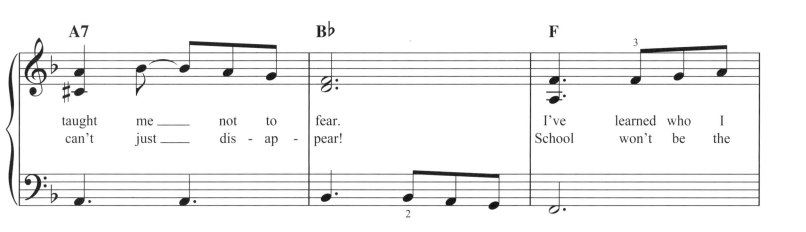

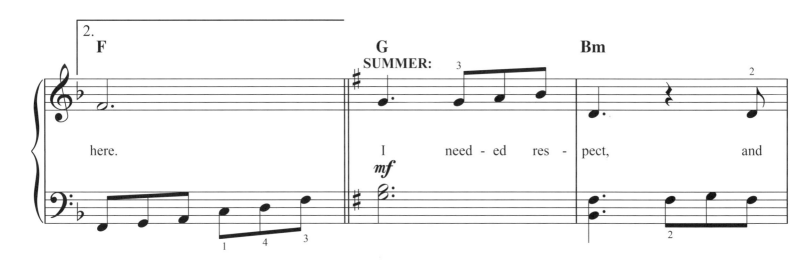

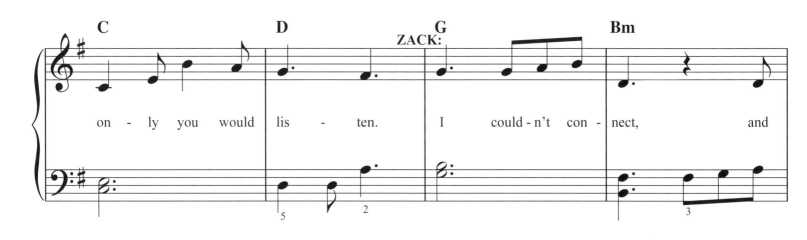

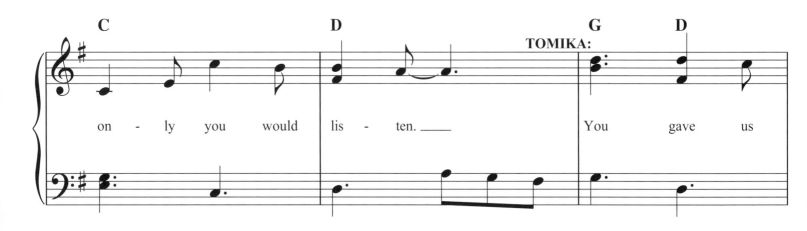

voic - es, _____ helped us _____ make them clear _____ You gave us

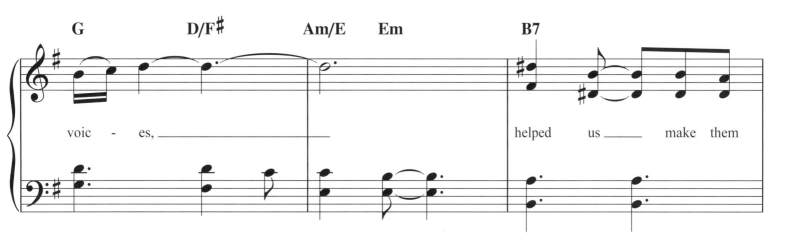

voic - es, _____ _____ helped us _____ make them

clear. You've taught us so much since you've been

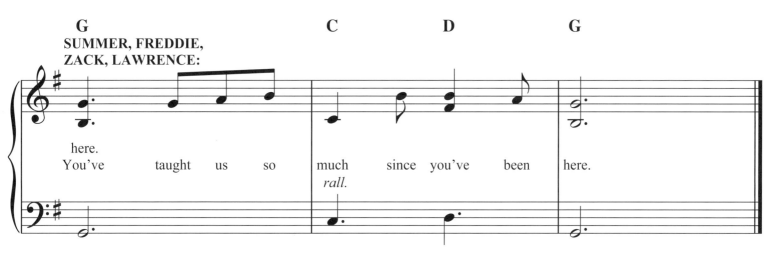

SUMMER, FREDDIE, ZACK, LAWRENCE:

here.
You've taught us so much since you've been here.

rall.

I'M TOO HOT FOR YOU

Music by ANDREW LLOYD WEBBER
Lyrics by GLENN SLATER

Power Ballad

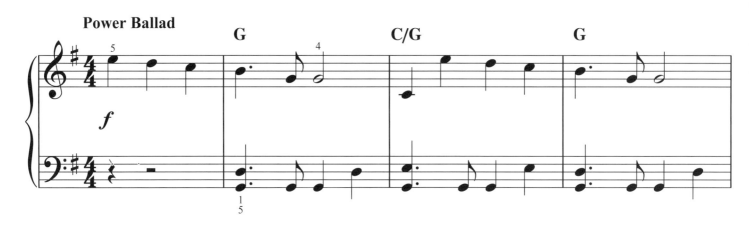

Girl, we've been to-geth - er such a long, __ long time. It's

been a great three days, you know it's true. But now I can't help think-in'

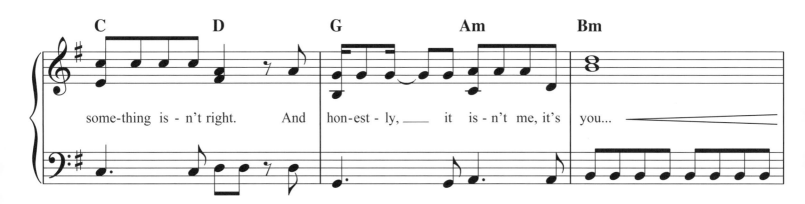

some-thing is - n't right. And hon-est - ly, __ it is - n't me, it's you...

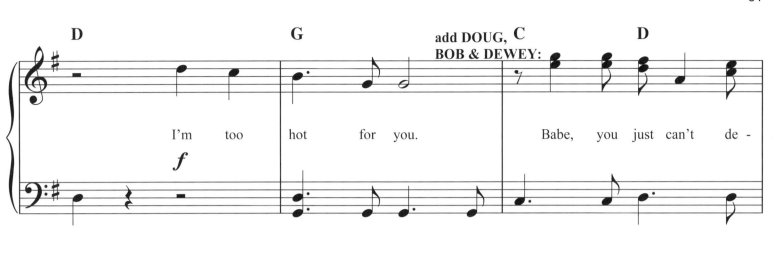

I'm too hot for you. Babe, you just can't de-

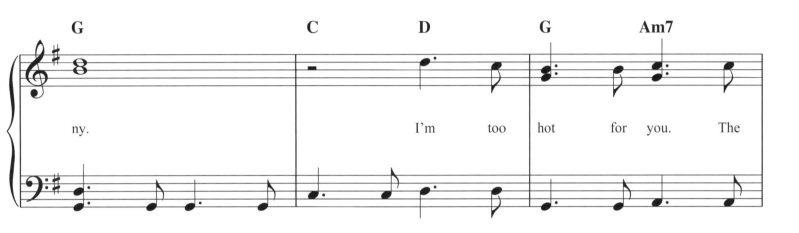

ny. I'm too hot for you. The

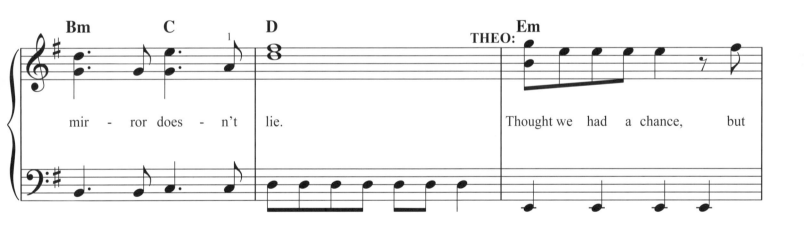

mir - ror does - n't lie. Thought we had a chance, but

now at sec - ond glance, I'm too hot for you.

So let's just say good - bye. Ba - by, don't feel sor - ry. I

know how hard you tried. _ I guess some things, they just ain't meant to be. Yeah! You

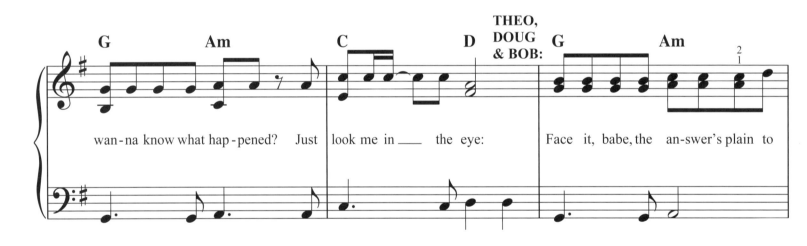

wan-na know what hap-pened? Just look me in ___ the eye: Face it, babe, the an-swer's plain to

see. Plain to see. Yeah! I'm too hot for you. Oh

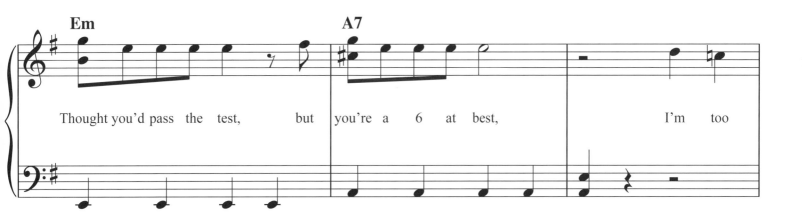

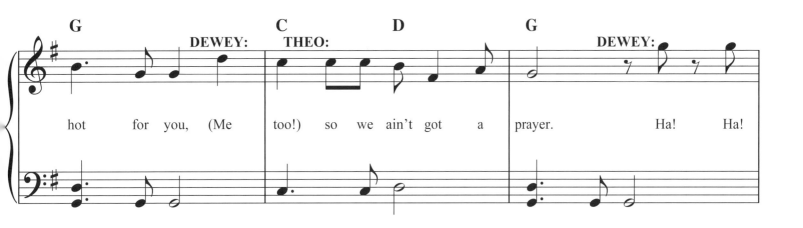

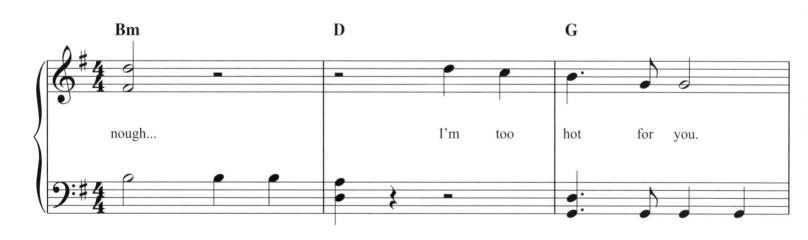

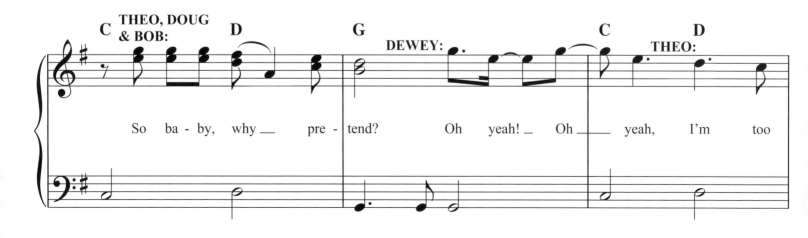

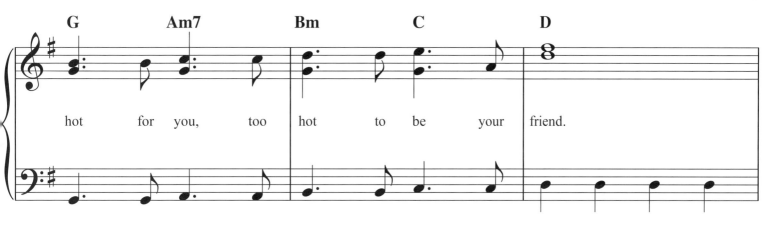

G   Am7   Bm   C   D

hot   for   you,   too   hot   to   be   your   friend.

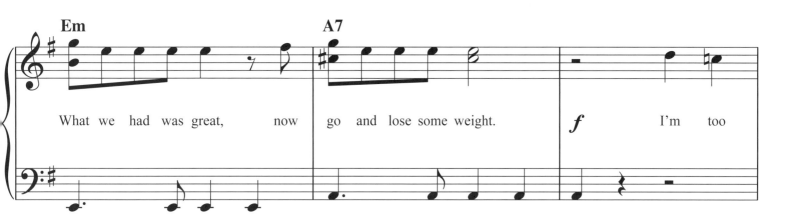

Em   A7

What we had was great,   now   go and lose some weight.   *f*   I'm too

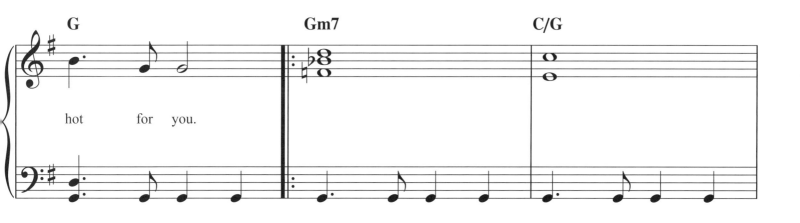

G   Gm7   C/G

hot   for   you.

E♭/G   G

SCHOOL OF ROCK

Words and Music by MIKE WHITE
and SAMUEL BUONAUGURIO

Driving Rock

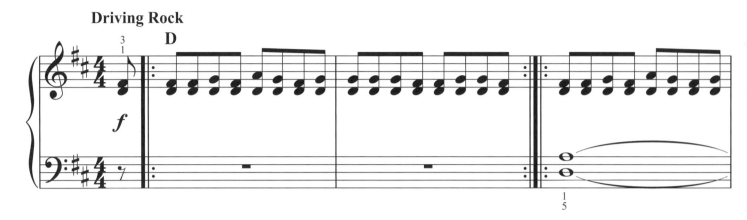

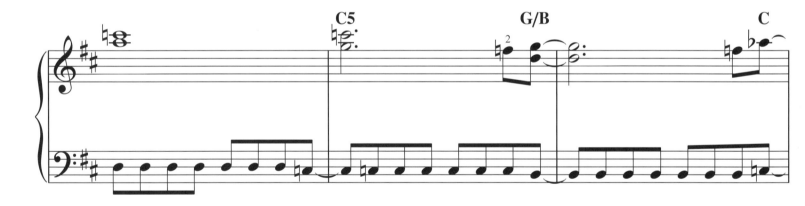

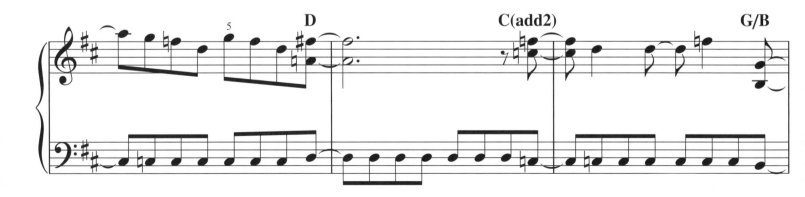

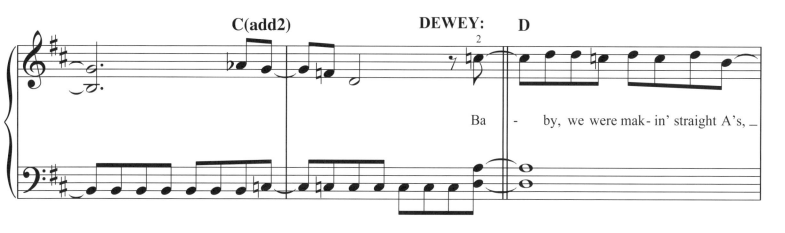

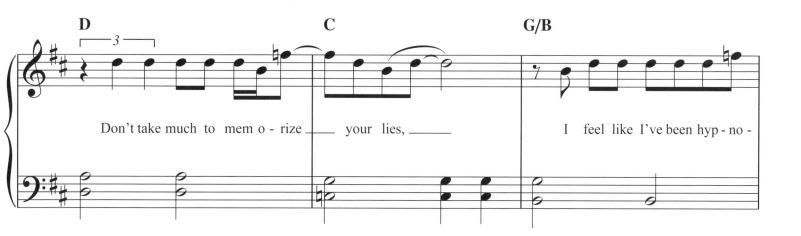

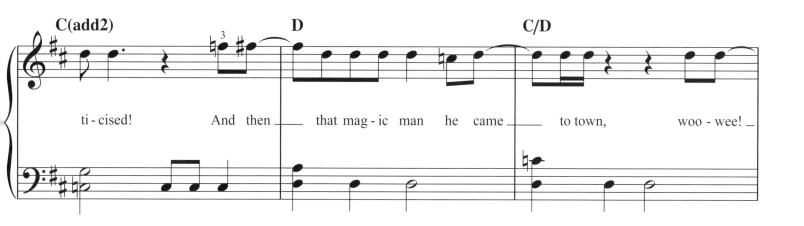

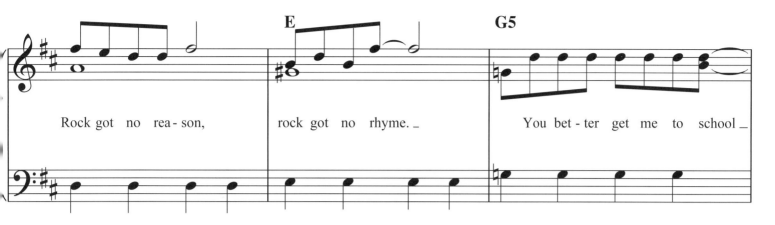

Rock got no rea-son, rock got no rhyme. _ You bet-ter get me to school _

_____ on time... _ Aw, yeah! _

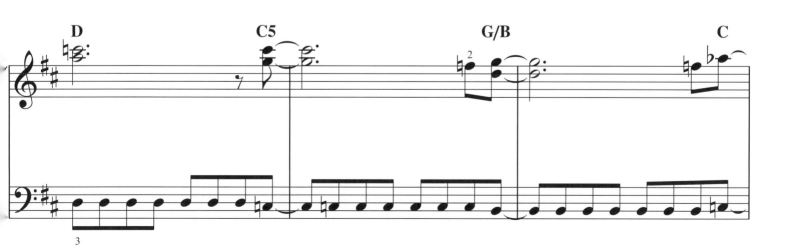

3

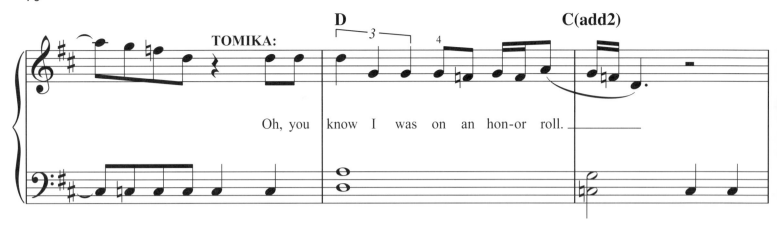

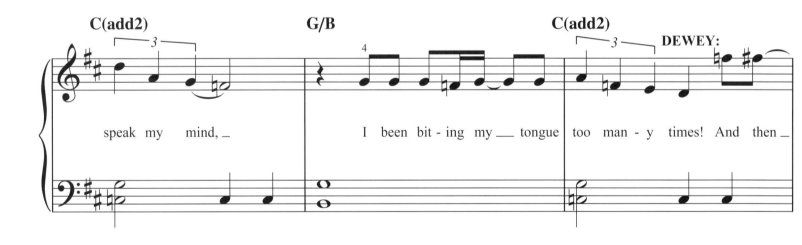

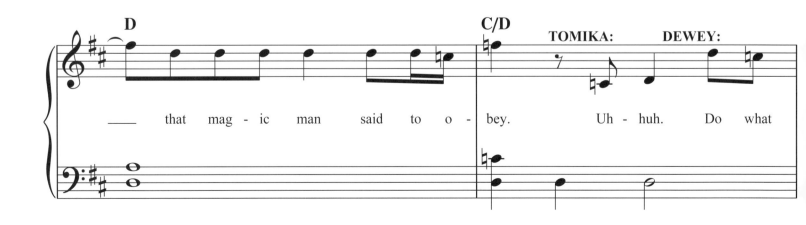

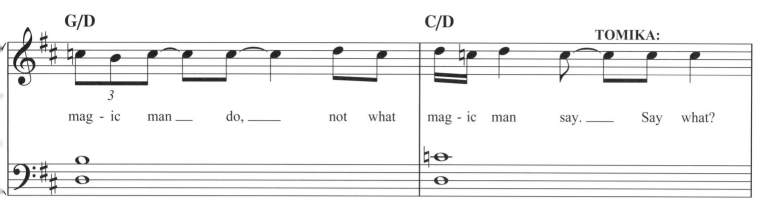

G/D   C/D   TOMIKA:

mag - ic man __ do, ____ not what mag - ic man say. ____ Say what?

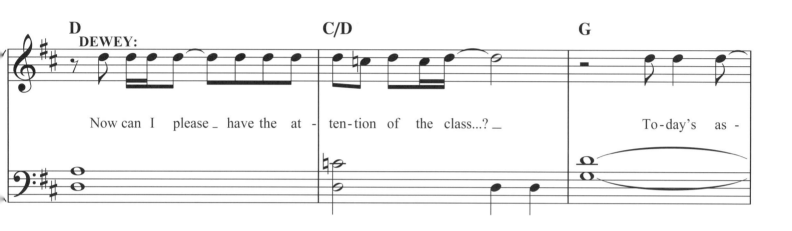

D   DEWEY: C/D   G

Now can I please _ have the at - ten-tion of the class...? _ To-day's as -

ALL KIDS: DEWEY:

- sign - ment...   Kick some ass! And if you

D   E   G

wan - na be the teach-er's __ pet, ____ well, ba - by, you just bet - ter for - get

D / **E**

it.   Rock got no rea - son,   rock got no rhyme. __

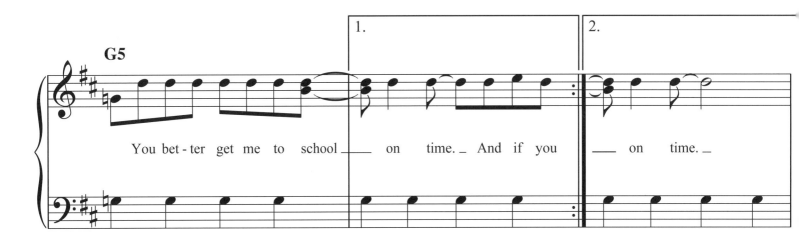

G5   **1.**   **2.**

You bet - ter get me to school __ on time. __ And if you __ on time. __

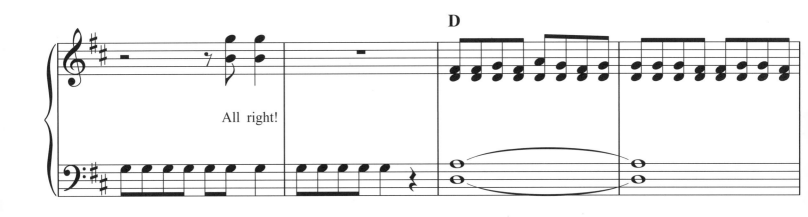

D

All right!

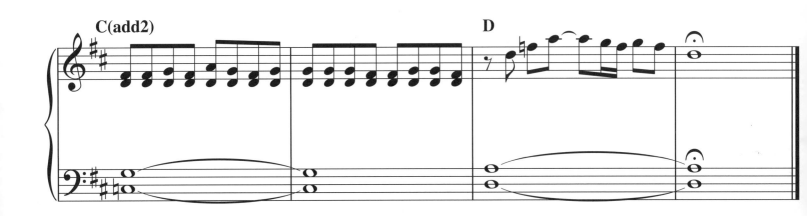

C(add2)   **D**